Susan Ferrier

Twayne's English Authors Series

Herbert Sussman, Editor

Northeastern University

TEAS 392

SUSAN FERRIER
(1782–1854)
Miniature by Robert Thorburn, 1836

Susan Ferrier

By Mary Cullinan

California State University, Hayward

Twayne Publishers • *Boston*

AAB9444

Susan Ferrier

Mary Cullinan

Copyright © 1984 by G. K. Hall & Company
All Rights Reserved
Published by Twayne Publishers
A Division of G. K. Hall & Company
70 Lincoln Street
Boston, Massachusetts 02111

Book Production by Elizabeth Todesco

Book Design by Barbara Anderson

Printed on permanent/durable acid-free
paper and bound in the United States of
America.

Library of Congress Cataloging in Publication Data

Cullinan, Mary.
   Susan Ferrier.

   (Twayne's English authors series; TEAS 392)
   Bibliography: p. 129
   Includes index.
   1. Ferrier, Susan, 1782–1854.
   2. Scotland in literature.
   3. Novelists, Scottish—19th century—Biography.
   I. Title.   II. Series.
PR4699.F4Z54 1984   823'.7 [B]   84–10767
ISBN 0–8057–6878–5

For my mother

Contents

About the Author

Dr. Mary Cullinan became interested in Scottish literature while an undergraduate at the University of Pennsylvania, and she continued her Scottish studies at the University of Wisconsin. Her dissertation on Sir Walter Scott led to the publication of articles on Scott's historical novels and to further research on nineteenth-century Scottish literature. During a stay in Scotland funded by a travel grant awarded by the University of Wisconsin, she began her research on Susan Ferrier.

Dr. Cullinan presently teaches at California State University, Hayward, and works as a consultant in the San Francisco Bay Area. She writes fiction as well as nonfiction.

Preface

The works of Susan Ferrier (1782–1854) were read by large Scottish and English audiences during her lifetime and remained standard literary fare during the nineteenth century. Yet she wrote only three novels: *Marriage* was published when she was thirty-six, *The Inheritance* when she was forty-two, and *Destiny* when she was forty-nine. In the long interims between novels, she lived a quiet life, taking care of her father and mixing occasionally in Edinburgh's social life. She never married. Although her novels attained considerable critical and popular success, they were published anonymously and only a few friends knew of her accomplishments. To the unknowing observer, she lived a life fairly typical of a Scottish middle-class woman of her day. But her eyes and ears were attuned to the foibles and follies of every social class and eccentric character. Her quiet decorum concealed a sharp wit, highly critical perceptions, and an acute sense of the ridiculous. Like many nineteenth-century women, she enjoyed a secret creative life shared with only a few select friends.

Susan Ferrier is important to the study of Scottish literature both because she gave birth to the first Scottish novels of manners and because her works express elements fundamental to Scottish writing and thought as a whole. She is also one of the first female writers to describe Scottish manners and Scotland itself from a woman's point of view. And her works are not just of academic or historical interest. They still retain the satiric wit and outrageous comedy that charmed nineteenth-century readers. Ferrier's sense of humor, her insights into Scottish character and life, and her use of Scottish dialect are equal to those of any Scottish novelist. Her writing is uneven, but at moments it is brilliant.

Ferrier's works are also of interest because they grew out of a unique period in Scottish history: the Scottish Renaissance. During these years the country emerged from centuries of war and privation to establish itself as a major force in Europe's intellectual and scientific milieu. In his work *The Scottish Enlightenment,* Chitnis claims that this Scottish flowering began in earnest by 1750 and did not wither until the third decade of the nineteenth century.[1] Edinburgh changed during this time from a dirty, provincial town to one of the most beautiful and elegant capitals of Europe. Scottish universities came to rival Oxford and Cambridge. Scottish inventions affected agriculture and industry throughout the world. Scottish literature was known all over Europe. Scotland's tourist industry began: tours of the Hebrides and Highlands were the rage. Among the great figures who appeared during these years were the artists Allan Ramsey, Henry Raeburn, and David Wilkie; the inventor James Watt; the philosophers David Hume, Adam Smith, Lord Kames, and Adam Ferguson; and scores of figures in all branches of medicine, art, and the social sciences.

The writers, however, are perhaps the most remarkable, and they certainly concern us the most here. Whereas Scotland had produced only a handful of notable writers since William Dunbar and Robert Henryson in the fifteenth century, suddenly the country was burgeoning with literary talent: Robert Burns, Tobias Smollett, James Thompson, Henry Mackenzie, Walter Scott, James Hogg, John Galt, Francis Jeffrey, J. G. Lockhart. Even Lord Byron and Thomas Carlyle were sons of Scottish soil. No longer was Scotland the provincial country for which Boswell had suffered so many cruel jibes. Within a few years it had become a major force in British literature, the source of the powerful *Edinburgh Review* and *Quarterly Review* and a host of popular poems and, particularly, novels.

Among the gems in this literary treasure trove we find Ferrier's three works. In the best pages of her novels, comic scenes, absurd characters, and lines of Scottish dialogue rank with the best of Scottish literature. These novels have a spontaneity and a charm often lacking in the prose of better-known writers. They capture, too, some of the most remarkable and humorous facets of a society that now exists only in novels, histories, and the letters and memoirs of the times.

Ferrier's works, like those of most artists, are products of the special time and place in which she lived. She was influenced by her friends, her literary tastes, her artistic milieu. She was, however, very much an independent character who did not consider herself part of a school or tradition. Above all, she wrote to satisfy herself. Tracing her literary roots is an interesting endeavor, but ultimately her novels must be viewed as works of art whose interest and worth are independent of external factors. Like those of almost any artist whose works are still worth examining after a hundred and fifty years, Susan Ferrier's contributions to literature were uniquely her own. Thus, the primary focus of this study is on the novels as individual artistic efforts which succeed or fail on their own terms.

While closely examining her works, this volume also studies the complex, contradictory character of the author revealed in her writing. A social satirist who yet clung closely to the conservative precepts of her society and church, Susan Ferrier never completely reconciled the divergent elements of her personality. The artistic results of these contradictions are manifested in recurring thematic patterns, many of which reveal an ambivalence about the roles and lives of women and the value of fiction itself. These patterns are similar to those we find in the works of a number of Ferrier's female contemporaries. Beneath the familiar tales of heroines finding happiness with gentlemen of fortune are disquieting scenes and images that belie the authors' faith in traditional values and accepted behavior. Unconsciously, Ferrier created works that question the established social order, and, in doing so, she became a forerunner of more overtly radical writers later in the century.

Ferrier belongs to a small group of enterprising women writers who profoundly affected the form and content of the nineteenth-century novel. But, despite the humor of her works, their timeless commentaries on human nature, and their important position in the history of the Scottish novel, they have been neglected in the twentieth century: the plots seemed timeworn to new generations of readers, and the sentimental and religious elements were unpalatable. One can chart the decline of Ferrier's novels by comparing the literary histories of Oliver Elton and Walter Allen: Elton's survey of the English novel published in 1912 discusses Ferrier in some detail, whereas Allen's short history of the English novel published in 1954 does not mention her at all. In 1924 Augustine Birrell wrote of her novels: "Devoutly as I hope that they are indeed classics, I cannot conceal from myself what looks suspiciously like the hues of old age, decay, and death. . . . altogether I tremble."[2] One purpose of this study is to bring new readers to her works: her three novels should not be allowed to die in the final decades of the twentieth century.

The author wishes to thank the friends and colleagues who have provided much support and assistance in preparing this manuscript. Many thanks are due, too, to the helpful and patient staff at the National Library of Scotland.

Mary Cullinan

California State University, Hayward

Chronology

1782   Birth of Susan Ferrier (S.F.) in Edinburgh.

1797   Death of Helen Coutts Ferrier (S.F.'s mother).

1800   Maria Edgeworth's *Castle Rackrent*.

1801   Death of Lorn Ferrier (S.F.'s brother) in Demerara. Maria Edgeworth's *Belinda*.

1804   Deaths of James and William Ferrier (S.F.'s brothers) in India. Marriage of Jane Ferrier (S.F.'s sister) to General Graham.

1808   Elizabeth Hamilton's *Cottagers of Glenburnie*.

1809   Beginning of collaboration on *Marriage*.

1810   Jane Porter's *The Scottish Chiefs*.

1811   Visit to the Scotts at Ashistiel.

1813   Jane Austen's *Pride and Prejudice*.

1814   Death of Archibald Campbell Ferrier (S.F.'s brother) in India. Walter Scott's *Waverley*. Mary Brunton's *Discipline*.

1815   Jane Austen's *Emma*.

1817   Marriage of Charlotte Clavering.

1818   *Marriage*. Jane Austen's *Persuasion*. Walter Scott's *The Heart of Midlothian*.

1822   John Galt's *The Provost*. Lady Charlotte Bury's *Conduct is Fate*.

1824   *The Inheritance*. J. G. Lockhart's *Matthew Wald* and *Adam Blair*.

1829   Death of James Ferrier (S.F.'s father); S.F. visits the Scotts at Abbotsford.

1831   Second visit to Abbotsford; publication of *Destiny*.

1832   Death of Walter Scott.

1846   Death of Jane Ferrier Graham.

1848   Death of Janet Ferrier Connell.

1851   Death of John Ferrier (S.F.'s brother).

1854   Death of S.F.

Chapter One
A Changing Culture
Eighteenth-Century Edinburgh

In 1782, the year of Susan Ferrier's birth, Edinburgh was a city teeming with changes. For seventy-five years Scotland had been formally united with England; but the rebellions of 1715 and 1745, bloody efforts to restore the tragic Stuart heirs to the Scottish throne, were still vivid memories. Toasts were still drunk to "the King over the water"—the aging, dissipated Charles Edward Stuart exiled in France. Nonetheless, the Union had brought some prosperity to Scotland, particularly to Edinburgh. By the end of the eighteenth century Scotland had increased its revenue 5,000 percent, while the population had increased only from about 1,100,000 to 1,600,000.[1] But with that prosperity had come a weakening of Scottish traditions and manners. In Edinburgh the distinctive Scots speech was being replaced by a more conventional English; the Scottish accent and vocabulary were still strong, but fading under the influence of "cultured" English speakers. The extreme sects of Scottish religion were dissolving under Hanoverian tolerance, and uniform judicial and political systems were replacing vestiges of medieval justice and violent political factionalism.

The city of Edinburgh itself was changing. The walled, medieval castle town was becoming a modern city that would later be termed the "Athens of the North." At first sight, old Edinburgh was—as it is now—breathtaking: the magnificent gray castle on its cliff, the Firth of Forth sparkling to the north, the green, sheep-covered hills to the south and west. But, on closer examination, the romantic aura of the old city disappeared. The city was smelly, crowded, and insanitary. Dark walkways, closes and wynds, lined with tenements, branched off from the High Street and Canongate. Often ten or twelve stories high, the tenements were broken into flats inhabited by dozens of families. Rich and poor huddled together; the poorest families inhabited the cellars, professional people such as the Ferriers

1

lived in the lower stories, and the nobility and gentry breathed the slightly cleaner air of the top floors.

Clean air was not a common commodity in old Edinburgh. Open sewers ran through the streets, where pigs roamed freely. At ten o'clock each night, when the bells of St. Giles's chimed, the malodorous household refuse was thrown from windows onto the streets. This gesture was accompanied by the call "Gardy loo" *(Gardez l'eau)*, but, despite the warning, many a passerby went home soaked from the liquids of a chamber pot. Walking on the High Street with Samuel Johnson in 1773, James Boswell lamented that he could not prevent his companion from being "assailed by the evening effluvia of Edinburgh."[2] In the same decade the Scots poet Robert Fergusson described the emptying of chamber pots in this city named Auld Reikie for its dirty air:

> On stair wi' tub or *pat* [pot] in hand
> The barefoot housemaids *loe* [love] to stand,
> That *antrim fock* [wandering folk] may ken how *snell* [pungent]
> Auld Reikie will at morning smell:
> Then, with an inundation big as
> The burn that 'neath the Nor' Loch *brig* [bridge] is,
> They kindly shower Edina's roses,
> To quicken and regale our noses.
>
> ["Auld Reikie"]

Inside, these tenements were crowded, dark, and more ill-smelling than the streets. The residents burned brown paper in the rooms to hide the foul odors. Due to the lack of space, servants were few. Every room had a bed in it. The maid of one well-known judge slept in a kitchen drawer; the servant of another wealthy gentleman slept under a dresser in the kitchen. Children often slept in a study, parlor, or even a damp cellar apartment where, claims Robert Chambers, they are said to have "rotted off like sheep."[3] Rodents and insects naturally throve in such surroundings: Lord Kilkerran stated proudly that his flat was "free from bugs" when he advertised it to be let for twenty pounds a year. If they had been so inclined, many residents might have turned the household rodents into pets, as did Susanna, Countess of Eglintoune: she allowed ten or twelve of her favorite rats to join her at mealtimes.

By the middle of the eighteenth century people had come to understand that sanitary conditions were closely connected with health. The city's death rate was appalling. Walter Scott's family was typical: six of his brothers and sisters died in their Edinburgh tenement, and Walter himself was a lame and sickly child. The miserable slums were not in keeping with Scotland's growing prosperity and with Edinburgh's position as the capital of North Britain. A new city was planned.

The New Town to the north of the medieval city was the grand project of the Scottish Enlightenment, the combined work of the most illustrious architects, planners, political figures, and even philosophers. Because it was meant as a residential rather than commercial area, the major buildings were Georgian houses and impressive public edifices such as the Physicians' Hall and Assembly Rooms in George Street. The wide avenues terminated in elegant squares. Gardens were everywhere. Fresh air circulated freely. The new Edinburgh embodied all the ideals of modern Scottish affluence, beauty, and order.

Middle- and upper-class families such as the Ferriers bought houses in the New Town as soon as they became available. With the separation of these monied families from the poorer classes, much of the spirit of the old city was lost. Formerly everyone had lived together: silk-clad ladies in enormous hooped skirts pressed by grubby streetsweeps, porters lugging coals, "gillies" carrying the day's water supply, bewigged judges, and a steady stream of tradesmen on the dark tenement staircases. Everyone knew each other. There was a convivial atmosphere, despite the prevailing poverty, or even because of it—for, since the depredations of 1745, many of the Scottish gentry were poorer than the shopkeepers. The camaraderie of the old town was heightened by an inordinate fondness for Scottish ale and boisterous night life which penetrated all social levels and contrasted greatly with the hell-fire strictures of Scottish preachers.

As the New Town was built, the gap between rich and poor widened immeasurably. The New Town was the Athens of the affluent; the old city became a slum. In 1878, Robert Louis Stevenson wrote that "Social inequality is nowhere more ostentatious than at Edinburgh."[4] Left to decay during a period when people were moving into the towns, the old city became even more populated, fetid, and unhealthy. It was not until the twentieth century that real efforts were made to restore the city, introduce proper sanitation, and generally improve living conditions. Now Edinburgh is more uniformly beautiful and clean than it has ever been;

but, in its transitions, it has lost some of the character that once
delighted all of Europe.

Edinburgh Society

Old Edinburgh was a sociable city—and it was a city of characters.
Rich and poor, male and female—the inhabitants took pride in
their individuality and eccentricities. Scottish idiosyncrasies dimin-
ished with the influence of the more rigid English society, but they
are captured forever in the works of Ferrier, Scott, Henry Cockburn,
John Galt, J. G. Lockhart, and other Scottish writers of the time.
For, as they grew up, these perceptive onlookers saw the Scottish
character, like Edinburgh itself, changing before their eyes. The
works of almost all the many Edinburgh writers born in the last
decades of the eighteenth century are united in their portrayal of a
society in flux and a world that was disappearing.

Due no doubt to these changes, Edinburgh society was a mass of
contradictions: it was both elegant and rough, enlightened and
dissolute, religious and profane. Despite the influence of David
Hume, most people attended the Presbyterian Church, which de-
nounced theaters and dancing; but taverns and oyster cellars were
rife with ribaldry and drunkenness. Cockfighting was a popular
sport with poor and rich alike, and an estimated two hundred
brothels flourished in the city. The young Boswell portrays this
night life more candidly than most writers, giving us vivid descriptions of the whoring and drinking that he and his cohorts indulged
in.

But liquor and prostitution are hardly unique elements in a city,
even one that professed the moral tenets of John Knox. What set
Edinburgh apart, as Susan Ferrier entered the world in 1782, were
its local characters, many of whom are still famous in the city today.
We meet them again and again in the letters and journals of the
period; and we see them, only slightly disguised in the novels of
social observers such as Ferrier. Boswell's Scottish accent amused
the patronizing London society, but he was not as eccentric as his
colleague Lord Kames and many of Edinburgh's aristocratic residents. Lord Kames, Lord of Session and an elegant writer on philosophy, literature, and law, had a rough Scots tongue that contrasted
oddly with his sophisticated pen. He once said of himself: "I ken
very weel that I am the coarsest and most black-a-vised bitch in a'

the Court o' Session." His last words to his colleagues, eight days before his death, were, "Fare ye a' weel, ye bitches!"[5]

Two of Lord Kames's colleagues were the judges Lord Gardenstone and Lord Monboddo. Lord Gardenstone is remembered for his affection for pigs, one of which followed him about town and slept in his bed. When the pig grew too large for the bed, it slept on the good judge's clothes, warming them during the night. Lord Monboddo, one of the most learned scholars and upright judges of the period, preceded Darwin in his belief that men were descended from apes. He maintained, moreover, that people were born with tails that were rapidly removed at birth by conspiring midwives. He habitually burst into rooms in which a woman was about to give birth in order to catch a glimpse of the baby's tail. The philosopher and historian Adam Ferguson was obsessed by the temperature of his house: he would throw his servants into a panic if he saw it had gone a point too high or low. He wore his fur greatcoat indoors and insisted on fur-lined half-boots and a felt hat tied under his chin with a ribbon when he went out.

In fact, every Scottish family seemed to have an eccentric in its midst. Walter Scott's grandfather refused to shave until the Stuarts were restored to the Scottish throne: his nickname, not unnaturally, was "Beardie." Susan Ferrier had only to look to her father to find inspiration for humorous eccentric characters, and her friends and neighbors furnished ample material for further fictional oddities.

Some of the funniest of Ferrier's creations, surprisingly, are female; eighteenth-century Scotland nurtured an amazing number of eccentric women. Such women did not flourish in the more structured English society; public censure of anything bordering on unseemly conduct, language, or apparel was too strong. But in Edinburgh, as Lord Cockburn wrote in 1856, "There was a singular race of excellent Scotch old ladies. . . . they all dressed, and spoke, and did, exactly as they chose; their language, like their habits, entirely Scotch, but without any other vulgarity than what perfect naturalness is sometimes mistaken for."[6]

Cockburn goes on to describe several of these women, some of whom make Ferrier's humorous figures appear more like literal reflections of the world than the result of comic fantasy. He tells us, for example, of Suphy Johnson, who always wore a man's hat, indoors and out, a cloth covering resembling a man's overcoat, worsted stockings, and heavy buckled shoes. Despite her startling frankness, her spirited conversation was welcomed in many elegant drawing rooms. Her father had refused to educate her, so she had taught herself to read and write as an adult. She had also trained herself to be a competent carpenter and smith, able even to shoe a horse. Francis Watt tells us that she played the fiddle, swore like a trooper, sang in a man's voice, and was believed by half of Edinburgh to be a man in disguise.[7]

The daughters of Lady Maxwell of Monreith were also famous for their eccentricities. One, who later became the Duchess of Gordon, captured one of the city's roaming pigs and rode it through the streets, followed by her sister, later Lady Wallace, who beat the animal with a stick. Francis Watt recounts an anecdote concerning Lady Wallace in her later years. When she told David Hume that she did not know what to say when people asked her age, he responded, "Tell them you have not yet come to the years of discretion."[8]

Many of Ferrier's absurd comic characters were copied so closely from their originals that Ferrier dreaded her authorship would become known. Her neighbors, the Edmonstone sisters, were instantly recognized as the absurd Miss Jacky, Miss Nicky, and Miss Grizzy in *Marriage*. And traits of Miss Menie Trotter's personality appeared in several of Ferrier's characters, including Uncle Adam in *The Inheritance*, who was also recognizably like Ferrier's father. James Ferrier was Menie Trotter's man of affairs, so, as a child, Susan Ferrier had ample time to observe the old woman's foibles. Cockburn tells us she was "of the agrestic order"[9] and would often walk ten miles at a stretch in very unfeminine attire. The oddity of this habit is highlighted for us if we remember how Elizabeth Bennet scandalizes the society of *Pride and Prejudice* by walking just three miles in "dirty" weather. Miss Trotter, like Uncle Adam, was a startling composite of thrift and generosity. Not trusting banks, she kept all her money in a green silk bag in her bedroom, available to any thieving servant or visitor. She once sent a present of fifty pounds to her niece by wrapping the note in a cabbage leaf and entrusting it to a woman taking a basket of butter into the city.[10] Each fall an ox was slain for Miss Trotter's meals, and she ate it regularly from nose to tail. Cockburn was present when she asked Sir Thomas Lauder to dine: "For, eh! Sir Thammas! We're terrible near the tail noo." She claimed to have had a dreadful nightmare one night in which she saw heaven filled with thousands of naked children. "That wad be a dreadfu' thing! for ye ken I ne'er could bide bairns in a' my days!"[11]

Many of the ladies of Edinburgh were writers, both poets and novelists. While they spoke their minds openly and wrote each other wildly entertaining letters, they published in secret, afraid to be associated with the dust of Grub Street or the stigma of profane literature. (Caroline Baroness Nairne did not let even her husband know that she was a popular novelist, Mrs. Bogan of Bogan.) The women of Edinburgh held a unique position among the women of Europe. They were not educated as carefully as men, but they were freer than their English sisters to pursue studies on their own. Susan Ferrier inherited this freedom. She did not enter a society with the opportunities of today, but she was born into a world that was flexible because it was changing.

Chapter Two
Early Years

The Ferrier Family

Susan Edmonstone Ferrier was an exceedingly private person who never sought the literary spotlight. She agreed to let her name be included only in Bentley's edition of her novels in 1841, thirteen years before her death and ten years after the publication of her last novel. Her grandnephew, John Ferrier, collected the correspondence that had not been lost or destroyed by the author herself; John Ferrier gave the letters to John Doyle, who edited *Memoir and Correspondence of Susan Ferrier.* Doyle's collection, Susan Ferrier's own memoir of her father, descriptions of her visits to Ashistiel and Abbotsford, and some comments by friends and acquaintances are all that remain to help us learn about her life.

The letters are a delight. Closely related in theme and tone to her novels, they reflect her character as it changed through the years. They reflect, too, the Scottish characters around her. Like her novels, her satiric letters capture society's foibles and vanities. As she grew more pious and serious in her old age, she became unhappy with her youthful commentaries and destroyed many of them; no doubt we have lost some wonderful insights into Scottish character and society.

What little we know of her father's childhood comes from her description of his early life. This memoir reflects her strong admiration of him and depicts his rugged individualism, which she inherited. James Ferrier's parents hid their affections behind a stern manner and harsh discipline. Left as an infant with a nurse during the Rebellion of 1745, he became, in a few years, more attached to his nurse's family than to his own. His parents, Susan Ferrier explains, exerted power rather than love over him, so that he far preferred living in the poverty of his affectionate foster family. When carried home to his parents, he would weep miserably or manage to run back to Nurse Barr. He continued to live principally with his foster family for thirteen years, suffering from the taunts of other children and the punishments and exasperation of his parents. Later he told his daughter that he had never seen a plentiful meal on the table during the years with his adopted family. At the Grammar School of Linlithgow, which he attended at the same time as his brothers, he suffered many humiliations for being the "son of Nurse Barr." She tried to keep young James dressed on the level of his brothers, but could not succeed. In fact, seeing one day that his brothers' shoes were brighter than his, she covered his with train oil to make them shine. The horrible smell that resulted caused him to be hooted out of the classroom.

James Ferrier's childhood was further marred by an accident while he was playing: he fell on a rusty nail that punctured his eye. Although he lost the sight in that eye, he retained good vision in the other for the rest of his long life. Being thus unfit for the army, the career his family had intended for him, he educated himself on his father's allowance of ten pounds a year and launched himself on a career in the law.

At twenty-three James Ferrier married Helen Coutts, the daughter of a poor Montrose farmer, whose beauty and manner had helped her escape from the poverty of her immediate family. When Helen was quite young, her aunt requested that the attractive girl come to live with her in Edinburgh. Helen's marriage to James Ferrier was considered a social step upward for her, but the young couple struggled through years of poverty, producing ten children, of whom Susan was the youngest. Helen Coutts Ferrier's disposition was softer and more convivial than her husband's; her death, when Susan was fourteen, was a blow to the whole family.

Upon getting married, the Ferriers first lived with Helen's aunt, then moved to one of the apartments in Lady Stairs Close. This was a prestigious residence at the time, having just been vacated by Sir James Poultney and his wife, Lady Bath. But, like other Edinburgh tenements, it was small, dark, and fetid. Even in her memoir, Susan Ferrier admits that it was later difficult to imagine the place as a desirable residence, "as the situation is now one of the most beggarly description" (*MC,* 11).

The family fortunes improved considerably as the children grew up and as James Ferrier established himself in his profession, becoming Writer to the Signet and working closely with the Duke of Argyll. In the 1780s the family moved to 25 George Street in the New Town, where they mingled with other well-to-do profes-

sional families and the Edinburgh aristocracy. George Street was—
and is—one of the most beautiful streets in the new city, 115 feet
wide, an elegant square at each end. Susan Ferrier's early life in this
attractive home seems to have been pleasant, although only a few
stories help us to reconstruct those years. As the youngest of ten
children, she was cared for by older siblings, and her father chose
her as his special pet. He was undoubtedly, however, the stern,
often uncompromising monarch of the family.

An example of James Ferrier's rule is shown in his treatment of
Susan's older sister, Jane, the beauty of the family. Jane was lovely
enough to have attracted the notice of Robert Burns, who wintered
in Edinburgh in 1786–87. Having met Jane, he addressed a poem
to her which began:

> Nae heathen name shall I prefix
>   Frae Pindus or Parnassus;
> Auld Reekie dings them a' to sticks
>   For rhyme-inspiring lasses.
>
> Jove's tunefu' dochters three times three
>   Made Homer deep their debtor;
> But gi'en the body half an e'e,
>   Nine Ferriers wad done better!
>   ["To Miss Ferrier"][1]

Jane Ferrier, besides being a beauty, was an artist and later copied
the carved heads on the ceiling of the King's Room in Stirling
Castle. The collection of copies was published by Blackwood, Scotland's powerful publisher, in 1817, a year before he published
Marriage.

Perhaps Jane's beauty and talent caused her father to insist strongly
that she marry someone worthy of her. More likely, since his wife
had died only recently, he preferred that Jane stay home and take
care of his household, as he later preferred that Susan do. For whatever reason, when Jane fell in love with the perfectly presentable
Colonel Graham, her father refused to let them marry until her
betrothed had become a General. Jane did not marry until 1804,
when she was almost forty and General Graham was forty-eight.

We see a different James Ferrier in his letters to Susan. She
brought out the softer elements in her father, and her special re-

lationship with him lasted his lifetime. His letters to her are often playful, and he addresses her by a nickname:

My dear Roe:

I think you must have heard of a scheme which some of my neighbours had in view of providing me with a housekeeper with one leg, if Jane had not fought her way through the snow, for you have only sent one garter which will not do for me, who have two limbs, such as they are. (*MC*, 26)

Discipline was strict in a Scottish Presbyterian household in the late eighteenth century, but the Ferrier children were happy in each other's company. Susan's siblings remained her close friends throughout her life. They understood her special brand of comedy, which developed early in the baby of the family. Two anecdotes of Susan as a child reveal her ability to mimic others—even her revered papa. One night, when her older siblings were secretly up late in the house, she startled them considerably by imitating her father's harsh voice. Later she upset her father himself by imitating the voice of an important guest, causing James Ferrier to rush away from his desk to greet his visitor.

Domestic Life

Susan's early years naturally centered on her large family. She may have gone briefly to an infant school, but otherwise she received a basic education at home. Like most upper middle-class girls of the period, she was taught to read and do simple sums; but the emphasis in her education was on drawing, music, domestic crafts, and "manner"—all enticements which could win a young woman a husband. At a young age she also learned the art of managing a household, for, as her siblings moved out, her father came to depend heavily on her.

Because she was often sickly as a girl, with a cough that bothered her throughout her life, she was sent several times to the milder climate of London and Tunbridge. Here she unconsciously accrued material for the English sections of her novels and acquired a breadth of vision and sophistication that most Scottish girls did not attain. She did not particularly enjoy these journeys, however, and describes herself in a letter as being "transported" to the south: "It is a dismal prospect to think of travelling six or seven hundred miles in search of health, which, for my own part, I don't expect to find" (*MC*, 50).

Her happiest times were with her family in Edinburgh. Her brother James was her closest friend; his loving letters display a deep affection. While Susan was recovering from her illness in England, James wrote her with tender solicitude from Paris, calling her by her nickname "Hughie" and signing himself "Moor": "Adieu, my dear, dear Hughie, write your own Moor often, and say particularly how you are. God bless you, my love, and with remembrances to my father and all at home, I am ever your own Moor" (*MC*, 29).

Since Susan grew up so attached to her family, separations from them were her greatest sorrows. Her life may be viewed as a series of losses. Her mother died and her sisters began to start families of their own while Susan was still in her teens. Her brother Lorn, in the famed Black Watch regiment, died in Demarara in 1801. In 1804 both her brother William and her beloved James died in India while serving in the Scots Brigade. These deaths, and others throughout her life, slowly affected her high spirits and lively wit. In her later years she turned more to religion for solace, and her writing reveals her concern with mortality and loss.

As a young girl, however, she had no outlet for her complex emotions except domestic and social activities. Her novels later recreated the immense boredom she experienced as an intelligent, lively girl relegated to the chores of a late eighteenth-century household. Again and again in her novels we see her high-spirited heroines tied to the inexpressible tedium of domestic and social life.

It is difficult for modern readers to conceive exactly in what all of these time-consuming household affairs consisted, for of course the Ferriers had more domestic help than most of us have ever had. But running a household was more difficult then: ordering supplies, sewing, washing and pressing clothes, maintaining silver and linen, cooking, and cleaning the house were full-time occupations for several persons. The Ferriers had a cook and probably a housemaid or two, but undoubtedly these domestics needed constant attention. Ferrier writes to a friend:

I have got a cook, a very bad one, but better than none, and I've invested her with all the regalia of the kitchen, and given her absolute dominion over the fish of the sea, and the fowls of the air, and the cattle of the earth, and over every creeping thing that creepeth on the face of the earth. . . . [Bessie Mure and Sir John] dined here on Monday, but they got such a beastly repast, and were so scurvily treated, that I've been sick ever since with pure shame and vexation of the stomach. (*MC*, 80–81)

Susan Ferrier did not openly rebel against the monotonous aspect of home life; only through her novels and an occasional letter do we see traces of bitterness. Her sense of humor helped to sustain her, even as the years went by and it became apparent that her life was not going to change significantly. "I am busied in the *Arts and Sciences* at present," she writes, "japanning old boxes, varnishing new ones, daubing velvet, and, in short, as the old wives say, 'my hands never out of an ill turn.' Then, by way of pastime, I play whist every night to the very death with all the fusty dowagers and musty mousers in the purlieus—and yet I'm alive!" (*MC*, 74).

Social Life: Edinburgh

The major occupation that kept Ferrier's brain active in her youth was observing the oddities of people around her. Although James Ferrier did not allow his family members to be excessively frivolous, Susan took part in many of the social gatherings of Edinburgh: the only activities for women outside their homes consisted of visiting their acquaintances and occasionally attending the opera, theater, or a dance in the Assembly Rooms. At these functions Susan Ferrier's eyes and ears were always busy recording eccentricities of speech, dress, and behavior. She writes her sister, for example, that she has encountered the widow Bell at a concert: "She came bobbing along, sticking out at all points and places, keys and *coppers* jingling in her pockets, led in triumph by a frightful male creature with a large *bow window* bound in blue and buff, and a pair of pea-green *upper legs*. I thought I should have swooned with shame when she stopped and stared at me" (*MC*, 36). In describing the Queen's Assembly, she leaves us with a memorable description of her sister-in-law, Kate Ferrier, whose costume made her the most conspicuous person there: "a dark lead-coloured satin (made at least six years ago, to the best of my remembrance), an immense black velvet beefeater's hat ornamented with large paste beads and high feathers" (*MC*, 38).

The social life of Edinburgh ladies, like that of London ladies, consisted of a great deal of visiting. Each visitor to the George Street house—and each visit made to neighboring houses—fanned the flames of Susan Ferrier's satire. One day she was forced to deal with two visitors simultaneously, the daughter of the Laird of Makdougall, a "great bumping lass in a blue riding-habit," and the good friend of the Ferriers, Miss Bessie Mure: "I was at my wits' end between a fine town madam and a *rank Highland miss*" (MC, 40). Ferrier loved her friends, but her patience was short with less privileged acquaintances. Madam Worm, for instance, was a "heavy handful": "She was in one of her vicious moods; she's a sweet *crater*. We're to dine there to-morrow, it seems, which I'm sorry for" (MC, 43).

A visit to Glasgow while Ferrier was still in her twenties only continued the tedious round of visiting. Even at this early age she preferred being alone to "being doomed to the society of stupid, silly, disagreeable people. . . . the nauseous *civilities*, the surfeiting hospitality, the excruciating acts of politeness. . . . I can liken myself to nothing but a hapless fly (mayhap a wasp) that has fallen into a pot of old thick stinking honey, where it wriggles and struggles in vain to get free" (MC, 56).

In the course of her socializing Ferrier must have met a number of eligible men, but there seems to have been no serious romantic attachment in her life. This was probably her choice. Although not a beauty, she was attractive looking, her fortune was acceptable, and she was known as an entertaining conversationalist. Her waspish wit probably disconcerted some potential suitors, but it must have intrigued others. There is a tradition that John Leyden, Scott's friend and fellow antiquarian, fell in love with her. But we have no evidence that Ferrier felt anything but friendship for that ungainly young man, despite his amazing energy and intelligence. Although born in a shepherd's cottage in one of the wildest valleys of Roxburghshire, as J. G. Lockhart tells us, Leyden "had, before he attained his nineteenth year, confounded the doctors of Edinburgh by the portentous mass of his acquisitions in almost every department of learning."[2] But, untaught and uninterested in social decorum, Leyden constantly surprised Edinburgh society with his uncouth manners and bellowing voice. While Susan Ferrier may have enjoyed Leyden's energetic and learned conversation, she preferred the more dignified, sixty-year-old John Philpot Curran, Master of the Rolls, Ireland.

Curran is the only man whom Ferrier ever mentions even jokingly as a romantic interest, but she speaks of her feelings so humorously that it is impossible to know how serious they were. One letter parodies the effusions of less gifted (or more emotionally entangled) young ladies: "He had the cruelty to tell me he liked me, and then he left me. Had my eyes been worth a button they'd soon have settled the matter; but there's the misery of being sent into the world with such mussel shells!! I (a modest maiden) said nothing, and it seems they were silent; and so we've parted, never to meet again!!!" (*MC,* 63–64).

Ferrier remained politely enthusiastic as her siblings and friends were married, but her letters do not reveal any strong desire to fall in love or get married herself. She poked fun at women who spend their time plotting for men and, in her novels, her heroines suffer sorely for giving in to their passions. When an acquaintance becomes engaged, she writes: "Wee Wynne is going to clothe herself with a husband, and such a one! Apollo is truly a God compared to him. Were there ever such a pair of little infatuated foolies?" (*MC,* 67). While still in her twenties, she writes to her friend Charlotte Clavering:

This is in revenge for your presumption in daring to talk of *love* to a spinster of my years and discretion. Know, Mistress, that I despise love and have no love for anything in the world except wooden men and acting magistrates. How can you talk to me of balls and dances, and drinking bouts—I, who lead the life of a saint upon earth, and eschew all such evil and vain pursuits? (*MC,* 72)

Ferrier's comic portrait of herself as pious spinster is belied by her obviously active social life and her delight in cruel satire and caricature. But her self-descriptions highlight aspects of her character that came to dominate as she grew older. As in most of Ferrier's comedy, elements of truth are not far from the surface.

Social Life: Inverary Castle

One of James Ferrier's most influential clients was the Duke of Argyll. Having first handled the Duke's legal business, Ferrier gradually became his man of affairs in Edinburgh. The Duke's lovely Highland residence, Inverary Castle, was a long, difficult journey from the capital. When tapestries or candlesticks had to be sent to

the Castle, or when a harpsichord master had to be hired, James
Ferrier was often commissioned to carry out the tasks. As the Duke
had a house in Edinburgh as well as on Loch Fyne, the Ferrier family
members became friends of the Duke's family. The beautiful Jane
Ferrier was a particular friend of the Duke's younger daughter, Lady
Charlotte Campbell. In fact, Lady Charlotte was responsible for
having Colonel Graham made a General, thereby bringing about
his marriage to Jane.

When Susan Ferrier was still very young, her father began taking
her with him on his journeys to Inverary Castle. These visits opened
her eyes to a new world: without them, her novels would never
have been written.

Life in the luxurious, if somewhat topsy-turvy household at Inverary
was startlingly different from the quiet, conservative, middle-class
existence in the Ferriers' house on George Street. Several generations
of the Duke's family lived at the Castle, and visitors were continually
coming to stay for weeks at a time. The area, then as now, was
excellent for hunting and fishing. The landscape would have been
unimaginable to a town-bred Lowland girl: rushing streams, craggy
mountains, endless moorlands, and the salty Loch Fyne. Although
she rarely saw the Highlands in later years, Ferrier cherished their
stark beauty and re-created it in each of her novels. Inverary Castle,
its inhabitants and entertainments, appear in various forms in her
three works.

The hospitality at the Castle was famous. Cut off from almost all
society but their own, the family and guests devised theatricals,
dances, and musical entertainments quite different from anything
Susan Ferrier had ever seen. She met the eccentric old Scottish lairds,
taking snuff and speaking in thick Scots dialect. She met the spoiled,
bored ladies of fashion and the mindless young people with plenty
of money and nothing to do. Variations on many of these characters
appeared later in Ferrier's novels. She even satirized the Duke's
daughters: Lady Juliana's traveling menagerie in *Marriage* clearly
resembled Lady Charlotte's and Lady Augusta's dogs, birds, and
other small beasts. James Ferrier writes to his daughter: "When
[Lady Augusta] comes there, do all of you take care to keep at a
distance from that vile monkey she carries about with her. Jacob,
her manservant, who was bit last year by her mad dog, is in danger
of losing a finger by a bite from that other favourite a few days
ago" (*MC*, 25). Lady Charlotte also must in some respects have

resembled Lady Elizabeth in *Destiny,* who loves only her dogs. Lady Charlotte's dogs were attended by a footman who made up their beds in her carriage.

At first Susan Ferrier was merely a quiet, wide-eyed child looking curiously at everything and everyone at Inverary. Eventually, however, she became a friend of the two members of the Duke's family with literary interests, Lady Charlotte and the Duke's youngest granddaughter, Charlotte Clavering. Although neither was as talented as Susan, they exposed her to literary people and ideas; and Charlotte Clavering became her closest friend.

Lady Charlotte Campbell (later Lady Charlotte Bury) wrote a volume of poems and several novels, among them *Self-Indulgence* and *Conduct is Fate.* The latter was published by Blackwood in 1820, although he had some doubts about its sales potential: "I hope the author will pardon me for the liberty I take in hinting that I feel confident that she could very greatly improve the first volume so as, in my humble opinion, to make it more acceptable to British readers, who are not accustomed to a husband knocking down his wife, nor yet to some other traits of Continental manners" (*MC,* 56). Lady Charlotte, in fact, was not one of the great literary lights of Scotland, but she surrounded herself with a number of them. "Monk" Lewis, famed for his astonishing novel *Ambrosio: or The Monk,* was one of her admirers and a frequent visitor to the Castle. He was also an enthusiastic force behind many of the private theatricals at Inverary which Ferrier later depicted in *Destiny.*

Ferrier's friendship with Charlotte Clavering was of far more consequence than her acquaintance with Lady Charlotte Campbell, for it eventually resulted in the writing of *Marriage.* Between them, the two young women devised the idea of jointly writing a novel and, when Ferrier was in Edinburgh, they exchanged spirited letters on possible plots and characters. Eventually it became clear that Ferrier's abilities in fiction writing were superior to her friend's, but Charlotte Clavering's critical judgment, as well as her enthusiasm, was essential to the creation of *Marriage;* her criticisms led Ferrier to improve the novel considerably.

Clavering's own efforts as a novelist were not successful, although Ferrier later tried to help her sell a novel she had written on her own. Charitably, Ferrier asserted that the chief problem with the work was its brevity: "its extreme shortness is its chief crime, and its excessive *personality* another" (*MC,* 93).

Charlotte Clavering's talents were critical rather than creative. She was also high-spirited and imaginative, more uninhibited than Ferrier; not only did she instigate the idea of novel writing, but she brought out the comic and satiric aspects of her friend's personality. Clavering came from a wealthy, luxury-loving family. She was impulsive, self-assured. The Ferriers were more serious, their lives not as carefree. No one had sparked the uninhibited facets of Ferrier's character until she met Charlotte Clavering. Her letters to Clavering glitter with wit and caricature. She scolds her young friend, sends her comic doggerel, and recounts all the gossip of Edinburgh. She describes the eccentricities of her neighbors and details the misadventures of day-to-day life: "We had Camillia dining with us one day in very tolerable state of preservation. She went next day to take, as she thought, another family dinner at General Maxwell's, instead of which she found herself in her rusty fusty worsted robes in the midst of a brilliant assemblage of powdered beaux and perfumed belles" (MC, 53). In these letters Ferrier is at her most lighthearted and cruelly witty; the writer of these letters is the same satiric voice that narrates the comic descriptions in her novels. One could say that Charlotte Clavering liberated that voice.

If Charlotte Clavering had had her way, Susan Ferrier would have spent much more time at Inverary Castle than she did. But Ferrier believed that her duty to her father was paramount; she would not leave him. Her serious sense of responsibility was stronger than her desire for pleasant company and entertainment. She speaks wistfully of "our delicious splashy walks at noon and our enchanting orgies at midnight" (MC, 56), but turns down her friend's invitations, even while admitting her own loneliness and boredom: "I'm doomed to doze away my days by the side of my solitary fire and spend my nights in the tender intercourse of all the old tabbies in town" (MC, 59). As she grew older, still refusing to leave her father, Inverary Castle became an emblem of an existence and a society that she would never know again. From her solitary place by the fire, she began to recapture them in fictional form.

Chapter Three
Intellectual Life
Reader and Critic

We have no specific record of Susan Ferrier's education. Being the youngest of ten children, she probably read in a haphazard manner, but never had a governess. Her father and her older siblings may have tutored her to some extent, teaching her some French and exposing her to the standard classics of English literature. But she never studied Latin, Greek, logic, and other subjects that her brothers were taught.

Probably her educational freedom was more of an advantage than an impediment, as Scottish schools for girls of that time would seem shocking to us now. Ferrier's brilliant contemporary, Mary Somerville (1780–1872), was sent to school for a time, but the teachers emphasized posture, not learning: "The pupils had to wear stays with a steel busk, and bands to draw back the shoulders, and a rod with a semi-circular contraption under the chin to make them hold their heads up. Thus encased, they practised writing, studied English and French grammar, and learned pages of Johnson's *Dictionary* by heart."[1] Mary Martha Butts's (1775–1795) education at home was similar: "From six to thirteen she had to wear a back-board with an iron collar, and did her lessons standing in stocks. Her food was of the plainest, and she was never allowed to sit in her mother's presence."[2]

James Ferrier did not impose such punishments on his daughter. A busy widower with ten children, he simply left Susan to pursue her own interests. She read most of the major writers of the time and became well versed in literature of the eighteenth century. Except in her correspondence with Charlotte Clavering, she does not seem to have shared much of her intellectual life with others. In Edinburgh she was surrounded by literary genius, but only her closest friends realized that her interests extended beyond domestic pursuits and satiric comments on her acquaintances.

As her reading progressed, Ferrier became an independent critic who paid little heed to public opinion; some of her biases now seem eccentric, but many reveal a sound reasoning and subtle perceptiveness about fiction. Her critical opinions were influenced profoundly by her belief that fiction and poetry should reveal moral truths. As she grew older, she held even more firmly to this precept, which influenced her novels as well as her letters. In *The Inheritance* her major characters criticize the "profane" works of Fielding, Smollett, Voltaire, Rousseau, Shakespeare, Burns, Thomas Moore, and Byron. In a letter written about eight years earlier, however, Ferrier asks Charlotte Clavering: "Did you ever read anything so exquisite as the new canto of 'Childe Harold'? It is enough to make a woman fly into the arms of a tiger" (*MC,* 131). In a letter of the same period she complains about *Emma,* although she basically admired Jane Austen and was influenced by her to some extent: "I have been reading 'Emma', which is excellent; there is no story whatever, and the heroine is no better than other people; but the characters are all so true to life, and the style so piquant, that it does not require the adventitious aids of mystery and adventure" (*MC,* 128).

She approves of the "good sense and truth" of Hannah More's *Coelebs,* but she criticizes it and Maria Edgeworth's *Fashionable Tales* with a perception she could not always apply to her own works: "I'm glad you like 'Coelebs'—the book, I mean, for the *man* is insupportable. He's a good well-meaning creature, to be sure, and is of great use in making a pertinent remark or hitching in a hackneyed observation whenever the conversation begins to flag, but farther his merits I could not descry. . . . Have you read Edgeworth's 'Fashionable Tales'? It is high time all *good ladies* and *grateful little girls* should be returned to their gilt boards, and as for sentimental weavers and moralizing glovers, I recommend them as penny ware for the pedlar" (*MC,* 65–66).

She did not enjoy John Galt's works and strongly disapproved of J. G. Lockhart's: "I have not read [Galt's] 'Sir Andrew Wyllie' as I can't endure that man's writings, and I'm told the vulgarity of this *beats print.* [Lockhart's] 'Adam Blair' is powerfully written, but painful and disagreeable to the greatest degree, and in other respects not fit to be mentioned" (*MC,* 157).

The Ferriers' family friend, Henry Mackenzie, was one of Ferrier's favorite writers. The late eighteenth-century audience loved Mackenzie's *Man of Feeling* and *Julia de Roubigné* because of the characters' intense sensibility and heartfelt feelings. But his novels corresponded closely with Ferrier's ideals for fiction because they were vehicles for moral truths; Julia de Roubigné was the perfect Christian heroine.

Ferrier's moral outlook, however, always clashed with her delight in the ridiculous. In one letter she even pokes fun at one of Mackenzie's daughters, who had been raised as delicately as one of his own heroines: "You must know his eldest daughter has been begotten, born, and bred in such a delicate, chaste, modest, refined, sentimental manner as baffles the description of a poor, ignorant, homespun maiden like me. Her father's Man of Feeling is a ruffian compared to her and Julia no better than she should be when placed alongside of this most sensitive virgin" (*MC*, 61). This modest maid, Ferrier goes on to explain, nearly swooned away when her little sister asked her what the word "bastard" meant. After much hesitation, she told the girl it meant a child without parents, " 'just like little Tommy,' " an orphan of whom she took charge. With great relish, Ferrier relates that at an ensuing party the child explained to the group that she was making a shirt for her sister's bastard. In theory, Ferrier found Julia de Roubigné the ideal heroine; but in real life Ferrier delighted in ridiculous situations that would have appalled the gentle Julia.

Although Ferrier admired Mackenzie's works, she did not let her friendships interfere with her literary judgments. Her affection for her brilliant friend Walter Scott did not prevent her from sternly criticizing his novels: "I've read 'My Landlord's Tales,' and can't abide them; but that's my shame, not their fault, for they are excessively admired by all persons of taste. . . . I thought my back would have broke at 'Old Mortality,' such bumping up and down behind dragoons, and such scolding, and such fighting, and such preaching. O, how my bones did ache!" (*MC*, 132).

One novel that Ferrier clearly enjoyed and that influenced her own writing was *The Cottagers of Glenburnie* by another Scottish woman, Elizabeth Hamilton (1758–1816). Published in 1808, this work is one of the earliest novels in the Scottish mode; although popular in Scotland, the novel appeared too long before the publication of *Waverley* to interest the wider English audience. Hamilton focuses on lower-class Scottish characters and effectively employs Scottish dialect. The graphic, homely details of the poor cottagers' lives are different from anything in the novels of Austen or of most English women writers. Although Hamilton's intentions were basically didactic, the peasant characters made Scottish readers laugh. The book contained characters with whom they were familiar, not simply elegant heroes and heroines modeled after English nobility. "Have you been introduced to the McLarty family yet?" Ferrier writes Charlotte Clavering. "I think they are the most exquisite family group imaginable. Mrs. McC is quite one of your darlings" (*MC*, 55).

Hamilton's work differs fundamentally from Ferrier's in plot, tone, and theme. But Hamilton's homespun settings and views of lower-class life, as well as her depiction of real Scottish people and speech, parallel Ferrier's in many ways. *The Cottagers of Glenburnie*, moreover, is told from a woman's point of view and focuses on themes (such as the importance of good housekeeping) that did not interest male readers of the time. Hamilton is the only popular Scottish writer prior to Ferrier whose works retain elements of both the regional Scottish novel and the Scottish novel of manners. Hamilton died two years before the publication of *Marriage*, and there is no evidence that the two authors knew each other. But *The Cottagers of Glenburnie* stands out as one of the few novels that met with Ferrier's critical approval and that clearly influenced her work.

Edinburgh Bluestockings

Ferrier lived in a small city burgeoning with intellectual life, and she was influenced by the new ideas and brilliant minds around her. But she did not mingle with the literary "set" of Edinburgh. Her friendships with the Mackenzie and Scott families were not motivated by literary interests, nor did they lead to much discussion of each other's work, as far as we can tell from extant letters and memoirs. Late in his life Scott assisted her in publishing *Destiny*, but that is one of the few literary exchanges in their relationship. Insisting on anonymous publication, Ferrier eschewed the literary limelight and did not consider herself part of a literary group.

Despite this intellectual independence, Ferrier doubtless knew— or knew of—many Scottish women intellectuals who had appeared suddenly in Edinburgh's small but distinguished society. Elizabeth Hamilton, author of *Memoirs of Modern Philosophers* as well as *The Cottagers of Glenburnie*, was a well-known literary figure. Eliza Fletcher (1770–1858), a friend of Hamilton, was a politically outspoken Whig reformer who had delved into Milton, Pope, Dryden, and

Shakespeare as soon as she could read. Jane Porter's (1776–1850) *The Scottish Chiefs,* an epic historical novel, which appeared four years before *Waverley,* may well have influenced Scott to finish his first novel.

Mary Somerville, born two years before Ferrier, rebelled against the strictures of Scottish education for women and became a brilliant scientist and mathematician, author of numerous volumes such as *Molecular and Microscopic Science, Connexion of the Physical Sciences,* and *Physical Geography.* Her long lifetime spanned major changes in women's outlook and goals. When she was eighty-six, she signed the Women's Suffrage petition, and shortly before her death she welcomed the foundation of the first women's college at Cambridge. Her name was given to Oxford's first women's college when it was founded in 1879. Mary Somerville was a feminist in the most profound sense; her life served as an example of rational, dedicated effort to achieve women's rights in a wide range of areas.

These unusual women were surrounded by many others, some with less talent, perhaps, but with an equally strong desire to pursue their scientific, political, and literary interests. Termed the Edinburgh "bluestockings," they were much derided by male writers and scholars. In *Peter's Letters to His Kinfolk* (1819) J. G. Lockhart describes the "infection of blue-stockingism"[3] in Edinburgh, sneering at women who discuss topics ordinarily belonging to men: "But what say you to the Scottish Blue-Stockings, whose favourite topics are the Resumption of Cash-payments, the great question of Borough Reform, and the Corn-Bill? They are certainly the very *flour* of their sex."[4]

Paradoxically, Ferrier, too, makes fun of such women. Her depiction of Mrs. Bluemits's literary circle in *Marriage* is even more critical than Lockhart's comments. Her satire allows for no middle course: these women are all absurd and vulgar. They have read Dryden, Scott, and Byron, but discuss only the authors' depiction of dogs. "It is easy, comparatively speaking," declaims Miss Pakin, "to portray the feelings and passions of our own kind. We have only, as Dryden expresses it, to descend into ourselves to find the secret imperfections of our mind. It is therefore in his portraiture of the canine race that the illustrious author has so far excelled all his contemporaries."[5] Lady Maclaughlan in *Marriage* is not a bluestocking, but she studies medicine. Ferrier presents her as a fanatic whose "cures" for her husband are apparently the cause of his perpetual ill-health. Her library includes such tomes as "Floyer's *Medicina Gerocomica,* or the Galenic Art of Preserving Old Men's Health" and "Astenthology, or the Art of Preserving Feeble Life" (*M,* 142–43).

Ferrier's attitude toward intellectual women points to a basic paradox in her character. Although she cultivated intellectual interests, she was ambivalent about the propriety of a woman forsaking domestic life for literary or scientific pursuits. At times she seems as embarrassed by her own talents and knowledge as was Jane Austen, who in one letter covers up her familiarity with the word *proem.* Ferrier's letters and novels expose fundamental contradictions: she loathed the trivia of social and domestic life, but believed women should accept the burden of their responsibilities. It is evident that many of the problems discussed by politically outspoken women such as Mary Wollstonecraft were deeply embedded in her consciousness. These problems appear in varying forms in her novels. But her religion, her environment, and her own character prevented her from analyzing such contradictions. She could deal with them only through the comedy of her secretly written novels.

Chapter Four
Adult Years

Nineteenth-Century Edinburgh

Susan Ferrier touches almost solely on her private life in the very few letters that are left to us. She did not, like Cockburn and Scott, record the public events of the times. Yet, during her long adult life which ended well into the reign of Victoria, she saw Edinburgh enter the modern age, and she witnessed many events important in the annals of the Scottish people.

Edinburgh, like other British cities, changed dramatically in the first years of the nineteenth century. The population nearly doubled, from 90,768 in 1801 to 179,897 in 1841, and the city expanded to the east, west, and south. The old city, as we have seen, was virtually abandoned to the poor. Middle-class residents moved toward the suburbs, and beautiful old buildings were torn down to make room for rows of shops and housing—middle-class tenements. The suburban sprawl was not always beautiful, but it was cleaner and more sanitary than the colorful old city. Plumbing was introduced—water caddies no longer carried the day's water supply to every house—and pigs and cows did not wander the streets.

In the first half of the nineteenth century, too, the great British railway system connected Edinburgh with the rest of Britain. The railroad considerably altered the face of the city and vitally affected the centuries-old isolation of the metropolis four hundred miles north of London. Now the rest of Britain poured into Scotland, and the Scots began to travel into the country that had annexed their native realm.

The Scottish people also began to go abroad during this period, for Europe was finally opened after twenty years of war. Edinburgh had been an armed camp since 1796 when Napoleon began his remarkable exploits. Men such as Walter Scott had drilled for years in their bright scarlet uniforms, readying themselves for an invasion. Many Scottish mercenaries had died abroad, and many Scottish children had lain awake at night, wondering whether "Boney" was

landing on their shores. In 1815 Napoleon's career ended, and the
Scots headed eagerly to France, historically their sister country,
which had sheltered the Stuarts and assisted them (albeit cautiously)
in their efforts to regain their crowns. In Edinburgh French fashions
became the rage—or the subject of censure. French ballet and opera
came to the capital. Exiled French royalty visited Holyrood Castle.
The influx of European and English visitors brought a new sophistication to Edinburgh; the city lost the last vestiges of brawling
sociability and provincialism that had been its charm and its
limitation.

A major event of these years became a symbol of the new Scotland—and the new Edinburgh: the visit of George IV. No Hanoverian king had ever come to Scotland; in the eighteenth century
a visit from George III would have caused riots in the streets. But,
although romantic nostalgia for the Stuarts still hung in the air in
1822, George IV was greeted enthusiastically. Edinburgh was in
an uproar for months beforehand. Buildings were torn down, Holyrood Palace was renovated, people from all over Europe pressed
into the city.

Historians have left us scrupulous records of the Visit. Edinburgh
entertained the king royally. As he rode through the streets, ladies
in bright silk dresses shimmered in every window. The Scottish
noblemen bedecked themselves in satin cloaks and plumed hats. In
a procession to Edinburgh castle the Lord Lyon, we are told, rode
an Arabian horse and wore a crimson velvet mantle "lined throughout with white silk; a green velvet surcoat, edged with a broad band
of gold, with a cap of crimson velvet, and a border of ermine."[1]
The streets of Edinburgh had never been so brilliant, glittering with
the trappings of an idealized medieval kingdom.

The coordinator of these festivities was Walter Scott: he alone
could have re-created the most romantic facets of Scotland's past on
the streets of modern Edinburgh. He filled the city with pipers and
kilts—the Highland dress that had no place in the Lowland capital.
He even persuaded the king to wear a kilt at the levee held at
Holyrood Palace. Scott created a pageant of people much as he
created pageants of words in his novels: he understood dramatic
devices and he manipulated them masterfully.

Susan Ferrier must have attended some of the festivities during
the king's visit, but she has left no record of her impressions. This
is a loss for us, for she could have seen much to delight her comic

sense. Certainly she would have seen the major drawback to the pageantry: that it was just a pageant. Kilts and ermine cloaks were not part of nineteenth-century Edinburgh. The king's kilt, worn over flesh-colored tights, did not fit him. The people saluted him because they were expected to—and because everyone loves a parade. Although the spirit of revolution was gone, the people did not love George IV as they had loved Bonnie Prince Charlie. These Scottish noblemen in their velvet finery no longer ruled a wild, independent Scottish nation; Scotland had become a subsidiary of England, tamed by prosperity and the passage of time. Edinburgh was not a royal capital and the king was not a sovereign whose exploits would be sung through the centuries.

The procession of George IV through the Edinburgh streets marked, as Scott intended it should, the solidity of Scotland and England. While the pageantry romanticized the past, it also presented a clear statement about the present. The time of revolution was past. The Scots could dream of past glories, but such glories were not for them. The modern age had arrived.

Publication

Whereas Walter Scott was fascinated by historical continuity and change, Susan Ferrier was interested in individuals, in the microcosm. Her letters recount the events of daily life, the meat of social comedy. She watched her native city move into the nineteenth century, but she immersed herself in domestic duties that varied little from one year to the next. Her father became more of a responsibility as he grew older, and her own ill health kept her at home more and more.

But she stayed at home also because she had discovered her talent, her gift. She could write. She had always delighted her friends with witty, satiric letters. Now she found she could create wonderful fictional characters, absurdly funny situations, and rich Scottish dialogue. Those dreaded social visits and wearying domestic chores could be intermingled with time alone at her desk—and they could actually be turned into comedy.

She worked slowly, for she was meticulous. And she worked in secret: not even her father suspected what she was doing. Her frequent correspondence with Charlotte Clavering kept her energy high and her ideas alive; nonetheless, eight years elapsed between the initial correspondence about the novel and its completion. By then Charlotte Clavering had matured from a giddy young girl to a married woman, and Susan Ferrier had turned thirty-five.

To Ferrier's amazement, William Blackwood, the publishing lion of Edinburgh, loved her book and published it in 1818. To her greater amazement, *Marriage* immediately became an immense success. Although *Marriage* could not compete with that other literary success of 1818, *The Heart of Midlothian,* it quickly became the talk of Scottish and English literati as well as of the general reading population.

Ferrier's success did not appreciably alter her life. She let out the secret of her authorship only to the closest of friends—many of whom had guessed her secret from the scenes and characters in the book itself. She continued her quiet existence and began to compile notes for a second novel.

The Inheritance was published six years after *Marriage.* The best-crafted of her works, it lacks the youthful spontaneity of her first creation. Perhaps Charlotte Clavering's marriage in 1817 accounts for part of this change; the correspondence between the two women became less frequent and less intimate, and Ferrier wrote her second novel without the spirited enthusiasm of her young friend. *The Inheritance* and its successor, *Destiny,* published in 1831, reflect the aging of the author and the gradual changes wrought by illness and loss. *Destiny* is even more serious than its predecessor; its plot centers on mortality and fate, but it retains elements of the comic vitality that first entranced readers of *Marriage.*

Ferrier's comic spirit blossomed early, then faded gradually throughout her life. Yet it is her comedy that sets her apart from the other writers of her time, for her novels capture Scottish life with a unique satiric wit. Some reviewers believed that her novels would outlast those of Scott, that her domestic comedy would prove more durable than his historical romances. This has not turned out to be the case. But in her novels we can glimpse a society that is lost to us now, and we can enjoy elements of human nature that will always be comic.

Ashistiel and Abbotsford

Ferrier did not use her literary success to make her way in Edinburgh society. She abhorred people who cared about social triumphs and catered to the wealthy and famous. She would never have become a friend of the city's greatest literary light, Walter Scott, had he not encouraged her time and time again. As the friendship ripened, however, it became one of the happiest parts of her adult life and clearly provided Scott with much joy in his last years.

Walter Scott and James Ferrier knew each other through the legal profession, but they were not close friends. The reserved, serious Ferrier probably did not approve entirely of his effervescent acquaintance, who combined his legal work with poetry writing and other frivolous activities. But no one could resist Scott's geniality and charm, and Scott admired and enjoyed his redoubtable colleague (whom he privately termed old Rugged-and-Tough). Scott was grateful to him, too, for Ferrier had helped his young acquaintance considerably when Scott was first appointed Principal Clerk to the Court of Session in 1806.

A warmer friendship grew up between Scott and Susan Ferrier. Their characters contrasted greatly, but they benefited from each other's strengths and enjoyed each other's wit. Scott invited James Ferrier and his daughter to visit several times, but they could not accept the invitation until 1811, when Scott invited them to his country house at Ashistiel: "We will take great care to give Miss Ferrier a comfortable and well-air'd room, and as we are near Melrose and some other showplaces, I would fain hope we might make the time glide pleasantly away" (*MC,* 237).

Ashistiel was an old house built around a medieval tower, to which occupants through the centuries had added wings and staircases. Behind the house were stables and gardens, and a stream poured through a nearby ravine. Three miles from the Edinburgh road, the house could be reached only by crossing a sometimes-treacherous ford. The setting was pastoral enough for a country retreat, but not impossibly remote, and the scenery was breathtaking: heather-covered hills and glorious views of the River Tweed.

As Scott's lease for this lovely establishment expired in 1811, he had arranged to buy another Tweedside property which would later be the site of his castle—and his ruin. He wanted James and Susan Ferrier to see Ashistiel before he moved to Abbotsford.

Susan Ferrier records the visit very briefly in her memoir, "Recollections of Visits to Ashistiel and Abbotsford." The stay was marked by ferocious weather: early October can be glorious in Scotland, but it can also be miserable. These days at Ashistiel were cold and stormy, "a perfect hurricane"[2] blowing through the valley. Scott could not, as he had hoped, take his guests on tours of his favorite places in the neighborhood. He ventured on some wet rides with the Ferriers' young kinsman, George Kinloch, but James Ferrier and the ladies stayed indoors through most of the visit.

Susan Ferrier does not give us her impressions of Scott's family: her memoir was written in later years, when her delight in drawing characters and caricatures had died. It is a pity she did not capture Charlotte Scott for us, as no one else has adequately described her. French-born, not intellectual, Scott's wife cared more for clothes and style than for books and storytelling. The Scottish playwright and poet, Joanna Baillie, one of Scott's closest friends, approved of her more than did most of his literary friends, but even her description is somewhat defensive: "She was very kind to her guests, her children were well-bred, and the house was in excellent order. And she had some smart roses in her cap, and I did not like her the less for that."[3] Visiting the Scotts some years later, the Irish novelist Maria Edgeworth commented acidly on Lady Scott's concern with clothes, mentioning particularly a cockatoo with scarlet feathers on a scarlet turban that she wore for an evening party in her own home.

Charlotte Scott may have been an odd consort for a world-famous writer, but her bubbly conversation probably cheered up the group of housebound guests put in her charge at Ashistiel. She did her best to entertain the Ferriers, taking them on short drives whenever the rain let up for an hour or two. The highlights of the visit, however, were undoubtedly the evenings, when the family and guests gathered together. Scott had also invited Daniel Terry, the well-known actor, and the two men provided delightful entertainments for the small crowd in the drawing room. Terry read dramatic scenes and Scott recited the old Scottish ballads that he had helped to bring back into popularity. Both were expert storytellers too, and they kept the guests laughing at a succession of amusing tales and anecdotes.

Ferrier, characteristically, does not give us any samples of her own conversation during this visit (sometimes one wishes she had a drop of Boswell's unembarrassed self-interest), but she clearly made a strong impression on Scott. As their carriage was being prepared on the day of the Ferriers' departure, Scott scribbled a poem for her that he later copied into her autograph album. The lines recall the stormy weather of her visit and ask her to come again,

> When this wild whirlwind shall be still
> And summer sleep on glen and hill,
> And Tweed, unvexed by storm, shall guide
> In silvery maze his stately tide.
>
> (*R,* 330)

Scott invited Susan Ferrier to Abbotsford many times, but, as her father grew more infirm, she did not want to leave him. He lived, however, eighteen years after the visit to Ashistiel, dying in January, 1829. In the fall of that year Susan Ferrier finally accepted Scott's "urgent request" (*R,* 330) that she come to Abbotsford.

Eighteen years had, of course, changed both Ferrier and Scott. She had visited Ashistiel as a young woman of twenty-nine; now she was forty-seven, bothered by a persistent cough and deteriorating eyesight. She was free to travel after all those years at home, but now her health and spirits prevented her from being very active. The journey to Abbotsford was a big event for her. And Scott was delighted. He wrote in his *Journal:* "Miss Ferrier comes to us. This gifted personage, besides having great talents, has conversation the least *exigeante* of any author, female at least, whom I have ever seen among the long list I have encountered,—simple, full of humour, and exceedingly ready at repartee; and all this without the least affectation of the bluestocking."[4]

Abbotsford in its own way was as great a change from Susan Ferrier's house in Edinburgh as Inverary Castle had been. It was the expression of Scott's happiest fantasies: it had been his dream, his passion. He had added considerably to the property, built a castle-like mansion, and furnished it with thousands of Scottish artifacts. After the publication of *Waverley* in 1814, he had possessed money to pour into his dream. He created the pageantry of old Scotland in his home, much as he created the pageantry of the visit of George IV. In Abbotsford he was no longer a nineteenth-century Lowland lawyer; he could live the romantic life of an ancient Highland laird.

In 1825 this dream had dissolved. Scott's financial indiscretions, the vagaries of the publishing industry, and a general economic depression had ruined him. In order to pay his creditors he began the superhuman work schedule that helped to bring him to an early death.

When Ferrier came to Abbotsford in 1829, she found the family sadly changed. Scott struggled to be his usual cheerful self, but he could not alter the mournful atmosphere hanging over the house. Scott's daughter Sophia, who had married the novelist J. G. Lockhart, was confined to her bed, and her son "Little John" was gravely ill as well—he would be dead before he was eleven years old.

Upon her arrival, Scott introduced Susan Ferrier to his grandchild Walter, whom he nicknamed Major Waddell after a comic character in *The Inheritance*. Then he took her on an extensive tour of his establishment, recounting, much to her bewilderment, the history of each dagger and claymore, each painting and manuscript.

Like everyone who knew Scott, Ferrier was charmed by his cheerfulness, courtesy, and generosity. She enjoyed his stories, his songs, his continuous good humor. But his antiquarian relics did not interest her, and she did not respond to the romance of the old ballads that "seemed to stir his very soul" (*R, 332*). She found his show of high spirits only accentuated his suffering.

Ferrier's memoir reveals the changes she had gone through even more than it reveals Scott. The author of this memoir is no longer a sharp-tongued girl poking fun at her friends and neighbors, exposing their weaknesses, laughing at their clothes and speech. She has aged. The loss and pain in her life have made her more serious, more religious. She wishes Scott's gifts had turned to "loftier themes" (*R, 332*); she finds him frivolous. This is the Ferrier who wanted her letters burned because they were too flighty—and who eventually stopped writing fiction altogether.

One night during Ferrier's stay, Sophia Lockhart was carried downstairs to meet the eminent painter, Sir David Wilkie. Delighted at having his daughter and congenial guests around him, Scott proposed that everyone join hands and sing

> "Weel may we a' be!
> Ill may we never see!"

Ferrier felt the unnaturalness of Scott's joy; he was trying too hard. His effort, she writes, "touched no sympathetic chord; it only jarred the feelings; it was the last attempt at gaiety I witnessed within the walls of Abbotsford" (*R, 332*).

It was during this visit that Ferrier asked Scott about some details of publishing transactions. With characteristic enthusiasm, he immediately offered to help her with her newest book, *Destiny*. He proceeded to carry out negotiations for her and, as a result, *Destiny* brought her more money than either of her other works.

Ferrier's visit to Abbotsford cemented her friendship with Scott. During the following winter she saw him frequently in Edinburgh. Visiting with him became some of the brightest spots in her somewhat dreary existence. "My chief happiness," she writes a friend, "is enjoying the privilege of seeing a good deal of the Great Unknown, Sir Walter Scott. He is so kind and condescending that he deigns to let me and my *trash* take shelter under the protection of his mighty branches, and I have the gratification of being often in that great and good man's society" (*MC,* 245). These are kind words indeed from the often acerbic pen of Susan Ferrier.

Doubtless Ferrier's sharp wit, as well as her perceptiveness and quiet manner, soothed Scott in his troubled last years. He repeatedly invited her to Abbotsford, but, after she had finally accepted, he was overcome by a paralytic stroke and her visit was postponed. When he was somewhat recovered, he again requested that she visit. Hearing urgency in his request, she accepted the invitation. She found him a dying man and knew this would be her last visit to Abbotsford. His voice had become indistinct and he moved awkwardly, rising with difficulty to meet her: "his face," she writes, "was swollen and puffy, his complexion mottled and discoloured, his eyes heavy and dim; his head had been shaved, and he wore a small black silk cap, which was extremely unbecoming" (*R,* 334). Much like her earlier memoir of her father, Ferrier's "Recollections" becomes a eulogy at its close. She saw death awaiting both Scott and his grandson, "Little John" Lockhart: "Disease and death were stamped upon the grandsire and the boy as they sat by side with averted eyes, each as if in the bitterness of his own heart refusing to comfort or be comforted" (*R,* 334).

In his biography of Scott, J. G. Lockhart describes Susan Ferrier's sensitivity during this painful time. Scott still endeavored to tell his stories and recite his ballads, but he would lose his train of thought, "as if some internal spring had given way—he paused and gazed round him with the blank anxiety of look that a blind man has when he has dropped his staff." Susan Ferrier on these occasions would pretend to be slightly deaf, telling Scott that she had not

heard a word since he said such-and-such. He would then be able
to pick up the thread of his story happily, "forgetting his case
entirely in the consideration of the lady's infirmity."[5]

The last paragraph of "Recollections of Visits to Ashistiel and
Abbotsford" centers on the ephemeral nature of human life, the
major theme of Ferrier's last novel. She lived twenty-two years after
Scott, becoming increasingly concerned with mutability and death.
The death of Scott was a particularly painful loss, for she had only
discovered the value of his friendship many years after he first tried
to be her friend.

Last Years

The strong bond between Susan Ferrier and her father provided
her with emotional strength during her lifetime. When he died, she
felt much of her life had lost its meaning. On the other hand,
caring for him had limited her life to a considerable extent. She had
refused invitations because he would be inconvenienced if she were
away, and her sense of duty toward him had prevailed over most of
her daily activities.

My father I never see, save at meals, but then my company is just as
indispensable as the tablecloth or chairs, or, in short, any other luxury
which custom has converted to necessity. That he could live without me
I make no doubt, so he could live without a leg or an arm, but it would
ill become me to deprive him of either; therefore, never even for a single
day could I reconcile it either to my duty or my inclination to leave him.
(MC, 59–60)

A little sense of her life before James Ferrier's death is revealed in
a summary she wrote to her sister: "We don't breakfast till about
ten, and at one I commonly take a drive to Morningside with my
father and walk about there, which, with seeing my friends, putting
on and off my things, and managing my domestic affairs, leaves
me scarcely a moment to myself." (MC, 203).

Probably Susan Ferrier's own inclinations as well as her filial
obligations led her to this reclusive life. Her eyesight was growing
poor and she was never in perfect health. James Ferrier, however,
must have been a cantankerous, demanding patient, and she let his
personality dominate her. No doubt the resemblance between James
Ferrier and Uncle Adam in *The Inheritance* was unmistakable: self-

willed, eccentric Scotsmen with occasional bursts of generosity and kindliness. In his *Journal* Scott tells a characteristic story about James Ferrier, calling him Uncle Adam and describing vividly the problems he provided for his daughter in his old age:

Uncle Adam *vide* Inheritance, who retired last year from an official situation at the age of eighty-four, although subject to fits of giddiness, and although carefully watched by his accomplished daughter, is still in the habit of walking by himself if he can by possibility make an escape. The other day, in one of these excursions, he fell against a lamp-post, cut himself much, and was carried home by two gentlemen. What said old Rugged-and-Tough? Why, that his fall against the post was the luckiest thing could have befallen him, for the bleeding was exactly the remedy for his disorder.[6]

When James Ferrier died in 1829, Scott wrote: "Honest old Mr. Ferrier is dead, at extreme old age. I confess I should not wish to live so long. He was a man with strong passions and strong prejudices, but with generous and manly sentiments at the same time."[7]

The Inheritance may help us to glimpse aspects of Susan Ferrier's life during the period before her father's death, just as it helps us to picture her father. Her second novel presents us with the satiric portrait of the spinster, Miss Bessie Duguid, the woman who has decided she does not want to be bothered by a husband; she wants to live a free life. As a result of her spinsterhood, however, she is constantly besieged with requests from married brothers and sisters, nephews and nieces, "all under the idea that, as a single woman, she could have nothing to do but oblige her friends. When in town, her life was devoted to executing commissions from the country— inquiring the character of servants, hiring governesses and grooms, finding situations for wet nurses, getting patterns of pelisse cloths from every shop in town, trying to get old silks matched with new, gowns made, gauzes dyed—feathers cleaned—fans mended, &etc. &etc. &etc."[8] Ferrier carried out similar commissions in her single woman's life: "I send you your gown, which I hope you'll approve of. . . . I sent a yard more, as it wasn't for a lady; by-the-bye, you should have told me what kind of person it was for, as there's some sizes between fat Fanny and Miss Wynne" (*MC*, 98).

In the days before shops appeared outside major cities rural Scots had to make great efforts to obtain anything they could not get from sheep, cows, chickens, and the rocky soil. Travelers to London,

Glasgow, and Edinburgh were always asked to bring back caps, gowns, shawls, shoes. But an amiable spinster like Susan Ferrier would receive an especially heavy number of these requests. No doubt she created Bessie Duguid in another effort to turn the tedious and unpleasant aspects of her life into comedy.

James Ferrier's death did not bring many changes into his daughter's life. She did move into a smaller house on Nelson Street, which alleviated some of her domestic responsibilities and was cheaper to maintain. We do not have a precise picture of her financial circumstances; her letters are concerned with money, but she was always frugal. No doubt she had enough money to live more luxuriously than she chose. She kept the same lady's maid, Mowbray, for many years, as well as a cook and other kitchen staff.

She took one trip to England after her father's death, but this was primarily to see an eye specialist: her eyes were increasingly painful in the light, and her sight was dimming. The visit to London made her eyes somewhat worse, however, and the boat trip must have been extremely unpleasant. Scott's daughter, Sophia Lockhart, invited her to go back with her by sea, but Ferrier declined emphatically: "much as I like you, and long to see you and Mr. Lockhart, I trust we may never meet at sea!" (MC, 251).

Shortly after the death of James Ferrier, General Graham died and Jane Ferrier Graham moved into the little house on Nelson Street with her sister. Although considerably older than Susan Ferrier, Jane Graham was far more active. She doubtless helped to keep the house lively with visitors and convinced her sister to venture out on occasion.

It may have been through Jane that Susan Ferrier met the artist Robert Thorburn who had come to Edinburgh to make a living as a portrait painter. Ferrier commissioned him to do a miniature of her, since her family had requested one. Her family was happy with the resulting portrait, although Ferrier herself never liked it. It suffered a series of accidents and was repaired by professional artists several times, so we do not know exactly what the original looked like. It remains, however, the only contemporary portrait of Susan Ferrier in existence. Depicting a serious, attractive woman in an enormous headdress, Thorburn seems to have worked more to capture her apparel than her character. We cannot glimpse her sparkling intelligence or wit in the face regarding us gravely from the portrait.

Although Ferrier was not enthusiastic about Thorburn's portrait, she found him very good company. He wrote her with some frequency and continued to see her whenever he was in Edinburgh. His reputation grew quickly. Soon he was exhibiting at the Royal Academy and then painting the royal family in Brussels. Success did not spoil him. He married a young Scottish woman and brought her to meet Ferrier during their honeymoon. He was one of the few guests who were truly welcome in the house on Nelson Street.

In her old age Ferrier was considered one of the last literary lights of old Edinburgh. She had outlived Mackenzie, Scott, Burns, Hogg—most of the great figures of the Scottish Renaissance. Visitors to Edinburgh wanted to meet Susan Ferrier, whose three books had become classics. The few letters remaining from her last years list a surprising number of visitors, but many times Ferrier was unable to speak to them, for her cough had become incessant. With flashes of her old ironic wit, she laughs at the visitors who come to see her as a relic and contrasts them with the visitors who come as friends: "H. Walker burst in upon me in the evening, with Miss Strickland waiting at the door wishing to be permitted (not to kiss my toe) but to shake my hand. I was so taken by surprise and so unable to remonstrate, that she was in the room and on the sopha before I knew where I was" (*MC,* 323).

Ferrier's preference for solitude in her last years was partially a result of feeling useless, the complaint of several of her fictional characters. After her father's death she felt her life had very little point to it: "my days pass away in darkness and silence, like shadows that leave not a trace behind. I lament my uselessness, and fear it must be my own fault that I am a mere cumberer of the ground, since none were designed to be such" (*MC,* 255). No doubt her sense of futility emerged in part because she could no longer write: her gift had gone. There are hints in her letters that she attempted now and again to start a piece of fiction, but she realized quickly that the voice of *Marriage* and its successors had been lost.

In 1836 her friend Hope Mackenzie, daughter of The Man of Feeling, had written her that a London publisher would pay a thousand pounds for "a volume anything from you" (*MC,* 268). But Ferrier responded that "I made two attempts to write *something,* but could not please myself, and would not publish *anything*" (*MC,* 269). Her acute critical faculty told her that she had lost her gift. As Ferrier's life closed in around her, we see her in her darkened

room, wearing the old brown dress that her maid deplored. Sometimes even candlelight was too much for her eyes, but she tried
nonetheless to read—or allowed someone to read to her. More and
more her interest turned to religion, which offered the support and
meaning for which she was searching.

In 1841 she took part in a "fancy fair" that would have delighted
the satiric eyes of her youth. The entertainment seems to have been
a pageant or masquerade in which "Eleanor was arrayed in a robe
of ruby velvet, with petticoat and stomacher of rich gold tissue,
head-dress à la Anne Boleyn," while others were in costumes made
of satin, ivy leaves, and similar extravagances. Rather than enjoying
the scene, Ferrier laments its artificiality: "oh! what folly all this
seems, and is! Not gaiety, real gaiety—only excitement, its vile
counterpart" (MC, 277). One is reminded of the pageant presented
by the heartless Florinda in Destiny: there an event that would have
been a target for extravagant humor in Marriage becomes a vehicle
for pious moralizing.

Ferrier attempted to live the religious tenets which she believed
so strongly in her last years. She gave generously to the poor and
helped her family and friends in every way possible to her. But her
tragic vision of life seems ultimately to have overcome and debili-
tated her. Her intelligence and sensitivity had allowed her to glimpse
the possibilities life could hold; but her conventional beliefs in the
proper life for a woman, daughter, and Christian prevented her from
living out those possibilities. She had not seen marriage as a salvation
from uselessness, and spinsterhood had not fulfilled her. The only
outlet for her energy and her intelligence had been her writing, and
that gift had somehow eluded her after a few rich years. She watched
herself become old, and, as the century progressed, watched her
books—the keys to her immortality—lose their freshness and vigor.
Even as early as 1844 Francis Lord Jeffrey did not mention Ferrier
in his essays on modern literature. "I am reading Lord Jeffrey's
essays with great delight," she writes, "notwithstanding the profound contempt with which (in the batch of novels of the day) my
bantlings are passed by. Not even a footnote to mark their existence,
poor things!" (MC, 288).

Jeffrey's silence was not altogether indicative of the popularity of
Ferrier's works in the 1840s. A new edition of her works published
by Bentley in 1841 had been well received by the public. Ferrier
allowed her name to appear on this edition since her authorship was

now an open secret. But her new Preface to *The Inheritance* reflects the changes in her attitudes toward fiction. She wishes she had "raised nobler plants in the wide field of Christian literature": "Viewing this life merely as the prelude to another state of existence, it does seem strange that the future should ever be wholly excluded from any representation of it even in its motley occurrences—scarcely less motley than the human mind itself" (*MC*, 280).

Before her death in 1854 Ferrier came to doubt even the worth of her writing. A woman torn by conflicts she could not resolve, she was trying to make peace with herself and the world, trying to understand her roles as a woman, as a Christian, as a writer. These conflicts beneath the surface of her novels and letters would become major issues in coming decades. Ferrier's unconscious restlessness and rebellion reveal undertones of the revolution of the future, just as they capture moments from an era that had vanished.

Chapter Five
Marriage

The Planning of *Marriage*

Susan Ferrier and Charlotte Clavering began to plan a novel in 1809. Their letters form a fascinating study of processes leading from germinal ideas to a published work; they also contain some of the most lighthearted aspects of the relationship between the two young women.

They first conceived of the literary work as a joint effort that would be carried out through their letters and infrequent meetings. Ferrier writes: "Your proposals flatter and delight me, but how, in the name of postage, are we to transport our brains to and fro? I suppose we'd be pawning our flannel petticoats to bring about our heroine's marriage, and lying on straw to give her Christian burial" (*MC*, 75). It quickly became clear, however, that incompatibility of style and subject was a greater problem than postage. Ferrier enjoyed her friend's penchant for sensationalism, but could not take it seriously:

What a glorious vision [writes Ferrier] burst upon my sight as I beheld our heroine, even the beauteous Herminsilde, sailing over the salt seas in an old beer barrel!!! My dearest of dear creatures, you must excuse me for having skipped over all the dry land and plumped in, heels over head, into the water, since really the barrel is as buoyant in my imagination as erst it was in the Archipelago. Methinks I behold the count and the squire *ramming* her in like so much raw sugar, and treading her down as the negroes do the figs, to make them pack close! (*MC*, 84)

Ferrier was equally unwilling to participate in Clavering's other suggested plots, which concerned the adventures of "men of the moon" and a "Hottentot heroine and a wild man of the woods": "I should despair," Ferrier admits, "of doing justice to their wild paces and delicate endearments" (*MC*, 86). In short, Ferrier writes that literary collaboration with her friend would be impossible:

You say there are just two styles for which you have any taste, viz. the horrible and the astonishing! Now I'll groan for you till the very blood shall curdle in my veins, or I'll shriek and stare till my own eyes start out of their sockets with surprise—but as to writing with you, in truth it would be as easy to compound a new element out of fire and water, as that we two should jointly write a book! (*MC,* 85)

Instead of a joint writing effort, the novel began to take shape along the lines suggested by Ferrier, her friend contributing criticism, moral support, and one chapter. The opening scenes of the finished work conform closely to the incongruous situation Ferrier suggested to her friend early in the correspondence: "I do not recollect ever to have seen the sudden transition of a high-bred English beauty, who thinks she can sacrifice all for love, to an uncomfortable solitary Highland dwelling among tall red-haired sisters and grim-faced aunts" (*MC,* 76).

Ferrier insisted throughout her correspondence with Charlotte Clavering that the novel must have a moral; her friend's lack of moral concern in her plots was one element that Ferrier found incompatible with her own interests. Ferrier was no doubt sincere in her desire to write a moral novel. She was deeply affected by the pervasive religious atmosphere in Edinburgh which frowned upon activities as frivolous as novel writing, and her penchant for comic satire was countermanded by her admiration for serious moral writing. Nancy Paxton suggests that Ferrier's desire for a moral in her novel may have stemmed in part from more mercenary motives, a wish to make the book salable and popular.[1] Paxton's conclusion is based on the following passage from Ferrier's letters:

Suppose each of us try our hands on it; the moral to be deduced from that is to warn all young ladies against runaway matches, and the character and fate of the two sisters would be *unexceptionable.* I expect it will be the first book every wise matron will put into the hand of her daughter, and even the reviewers will relax of their severity in favour of the morality of this little work. (*MC,* 76)

From the tone of this passage and from an examination of Ferrier's general moral outlook, it would seem that she is assuming an ironic and comical attitude when she speaks of using the moral message to assuage critics and gain a readership. There is, no doubt, a grain of truth in her observation of the vagaries of the literary world; but

Paxton's conclusion that Ferrier is not seriously concerned about a moral message in her writing contradicts a fundamental aspect of Ferrier's character that takes traditional morality very seriously, even while her ironic vision distances her from that morality and enables her to take liberties with it.

In order to live up to Ferrier's moral expectations, Charlotte Clavering smothered her inclinations toward the sensational and bizarre and wrote a very moral chapter for *Marriage*, "The History of Mrs. Douglas," a set-piece that entirely lacks the liveliness and color of Clavering's letters. It is, as she herself admitted, "the only few pages that will be skipped" (*MC*, 133). Without the cruel wit and absurd characters of Ferrier's writing, Clavering's chapter is a flat tale of fashionable life, no worse or better than chapters in many second-rate novels of manners.

Although Charlotte Clavering did not contribute substantially to the writing of *Marriage*, she helped considerably in her role as editor and critic. "If any reader," writes John Doyle, "takes the trouble to go through [Charlotte Clavering's] letter of May 10, 1813, and to compare 'Marriage' as we actually have it, with 'Marriage' as she criticizes it, they will see how much Miss Ferrier owed to her friend's advice" (*MC*, 48). Clavering's discourse on "high life" dialogue is particularly acute. She perceives that the conversations of the upper-class characters in *Marriage* are not realistic; "they are," she writes, "a sort of thing by consent handed down from generation to generation in novels, but have little or no groundwork in truth" (*MC*, 115). No doubt Ferrier modified her draft considerably as a result of this letter—unfortunately the manuscript is not extant. She must have altered the time sequence of the novel so it does not end some years after the date of its publication; she probably took out some of the French phrases in Juliana's conversation as well. Clavering's letter is so perceptive that one feels her desire to be a novelist was unfortunate: she was a born critic.

Charlotte Clavering's inability to take an active part in the actual writing of *Marriage* may have been a major factor in delaying the publication of the novel. *Marriage* was not submitted to William Blackwood until 1817, eight years after the literary collaboration began. It was finally published anonymously in 1818. The initial planning took place five years before Scott published his first novel; by 1818 Britain was deep in the throes of *Waverley* madness—a fact which must have made Blackwood's decision to publish *Marriage* a relatively easy one, but which certainly detracted from its popular reception.

The question of why Ferrier waited so long to finish and publish her work remains unanswered. No doubt Clavering's lack of writing skill contributed to the delay, as did Ferrier's fear that her satiric caricatures could be easily recognized. Her hesitation may also have stemmed in part from her ambivalence toward comic novels and toward her own literary talents. She was, moreover, a slow and careful writer who never scribbled anything in a hurry except, perhaps, an occasional letter.

Ferrier's fear of reprisals, if it did not actually cause her to delay publication, did become a major factor in her decision to publish *Marriage* anonymously. She wrote Clavering: "if we engage in this undertaking, let it be kept a profound secret from every human being. If I was suspected of being accessory to such foul deeds my brothers and sisters would murder me, and my father bury me alive" (*MC*, 77). Anonymous publications, however, were very common at that time, even by writers who would never be sued for libel. After all, the identity of the "Author of Waverley" was still undisclosed. Women especially were reluctant to expose themselves to the publicity of literary life and to the tinge of immorality associated with novel writing. As *Marriage* was immediately successful, Ferrier rejoiced that she did not have to bear personally the burden of public criticism and praise. She could continue her private life in Edinburgh and began slowly turning her thoughts toward *The Inheritance*.

Reception of *Marriage*

The story of old Mr. Ferrier's reaction to *Marriage* is worth repeating. Both W. M. Parker and Aline Grant tell the tale without demur, but John Doyle admits that it resembles one told about Fanny Burney. Nonetheless, the story goes that, as her father thoroughly disliked books by women writers, Susan Ferrier read her manuscript of *Marriage* to him from behind the curtains of his bed while he was ill. When she was done, he requested another book by the same author, claiming it was the best book she had ever brought him. When his daughter revealed the author's name, he was incredulous. Only the manuscript, so the story concludes, finally convinced him of his daughter's genius. The appeal of the story lies partly in that, from what we know of old James Ferrier, it sounds very like him.

The story also captures the enthusiasm with which many critics received *Marriage*. Blackwood's investment of a hundred fifty pounds was a remunerative one. When he received the novel, which Ferrier had first entitled *The Chiefs of Glenfern*, Blackwood wrote to her: "The whole construction and execution appear . . . so admirable that it would almost be presumption in any one to offer corrections to such a writer" (*MC*, 138–39). The most famous comment on *Marriage* was made by Walter Scott, in his guise as the Author of Waverley, in the Epilogue to *The Legend of Montrose:*

I retire from the [literary] field, conscious that there remains behind not only a large harvest, but labourers capable of gathering it in. More than one writer has of late displayed talents of this description; and if the present author, himself a phantom, may be permitted to distinguish a brother, or perhaps a sister shadow, he would mention in particular, the author of the very lively work entitled "Marriage."[2]

As the Author of Waverley was at this time the lion of all Europe as well as of Britain, this was strong praise. And it was disinterested praise, for, although James Ferrier was a colleague of Scott's, there is no evidence that Scott knew the authorship of *Marriage* until much later.

Scottish readers loved *Marriage*. W. M. Parker claims that:

Not only did Edinburgh enjoy *Marriage*, for instance, as something new in contemporary fiction, but it discussed the book with animation at interminable bluestocking tea-parties, trying to identify the characters. Lady MacLaughlan must be Mrs. Dames, the sculptor, or Aunts Grizzy, Jacky, and Nicky were recognizable as the Misses Edmonstone of George Street, distantly related to the Duke of Argyll, and so on.[3]

John Doyle quotes the inestimable Mrs. Piozzi, Samuel Johnson's longtime friend, who wrote Sir James Fellowes in 1818: "Meanwhile ladies leave cards and starving females write romances. The novel called 'Marriage' is the newest and merriest. How marriage should be a new thing, that is at least as old as Adam, the author may tell: but 'tis a very comical thing, and would make Lady Fellowes laugh on a long evening" (*MC*, 146). Of Ferrier's acquaintances, only Monk Lewis, in his capricious manner, condemned *Marriage*. He criticized the work, however, before he had even seen it; in fact, he died before returning to Britain from Jamaica the year it was published. He writes in fussy consternation to Lady Charlotte Campbell:

I hear it rumored that Miss F-r doth write novels, or is about writing one. I wish she would leave such nonsense alone, for however great a respect I may entertain for her talents (which I do), I tremble lest she should fail in this book-making and as a rule I have an aversion, a pity and contempt for all female scribblers . . . [I am] at the present moment much enraged at Lady— for having come out in the shape of a novel, and now hearing that Miss F-r is about to follow her bad example, I write in great perturbation of mind, and cannot think or speak of anything else.[4]

The pervasive moralizing elements in *Marriage* that have contributed to its obscurity in the twentieth century were not distressing to readers in 1818; in fact, many readers and critics admired the author's high-mindedness. William Blackwood, knowledgeable in what would sell, particularly praises the characters most modern readers find overly sentimental and pietistic: "Every one has felt in youth the glow of enthusiasm so well pourtrayed in Mary" (*MC*, 139). "Your picture of the blind mother and her son," he goes on to note, "is most striking" (*MC*, 140–41). Even as late as 1842 a critic for the *Edinburgh Review* described Ferrier as "one who has added so much to our picture gallery of original characters, and enlarged the boundaries of innocent enjoyment, without admitting an image or a sentiment which even a Christian moralist could disapprove."[5] As the century progressed, however, changing attitudes adversely affected the critics' reactions to Ferrier's combinations of comedy and moral comment: "unhappily," writes a critic for *Macmillan's* in 1898, "she was possessed with the desire to convey moral instruction, and that has overlaid her humour and her genuine faculty of creation with a dead weight of platitudes under which they must inevitably sink."[6]

Scott's novels, as has been mentioned, were both helpful and detrimental to *Marriage*. Some readers conjectured that the Author of Waverley was the author of *Marriage:* in the madness of Scott's popularity, any fiction with a Scottish setting was held by someone to be the work of the Lion of the North. As Wendy Craik writes, "it would have been much to Miss Ferrier's advantage if Sir Walter Scott had stuck to poetry and never turned his mind to novel-writing."[7] But at least one critic—the writer for the *Edinburgh*

Review quoted above, averred that readers would tire of Scott and would find Ferrier's fiction more enduring:

" . . . and now that the fascination produced by his genius has settled into a more sober, though not less deep feeling of admiration, and that the world has grown somewhat weary of the pomp and circumstance of chivalrous and historical pageants . . . the solid but unobtrusive excellences of [Ferrier's] novels will appear more and more conspicuous, as the stars come out with an independent lustre when the sun retires.[8]

Clearly this critic's prediction has not proved accurate; the historical pageantry of the Waverley Novels *has* lost much of its popular appeal in the twentieth century, but Scott's novels are still reread and reprinted. Ferrier's "more sober and homely order" of fiction[9] is known to only the most ardent students of Scottish literature.

There is no doubt that *Marriage* is an uneven work. Ferrier would be the first to admit that she was not attempting to rival Scott's powers. But *Marriage* possesses a vitality, an earthiness, and a sense of humor ranging from the madcap to the cruelly satiric that are unsurpassed by any British woman novelist before her. We smile, even chuckle, at Austen's Mrs. Bennet and her marriageable daughters, but we laugh outright at Ferrier's five awkward "purple" girls and their long-chinned aunts. Austen delights us with the subtlety and precision with which she unravels her characters' errors and follies; Ferrier makes us laugh by her ruthless expositions of her human creations. She pushes them heartlessly into the most incongruous situations and magnifies their follies until they envelop the characters' whole being. Ferrier's satire and wit are without pity. Her characters are unable to change: they will remain gluttons, flirts, bores, or busybodies until they die. The reader cannot sympathize with them—and he or she is probably laughing too hard to *want* to sympathize with them.

Structure

Marriage brings together the histories of two generations and moves between two major settings; this flexible structure allows ample room for humorous anecdotes and characters of all kinds. "Of story," wrote one critic, "[*Marriage*] had as little as the knife-grinder."[10] This is an exaggeration as is, to some degree, Saintsbury's comment on the story line: "This second volume [of *Marriage*] includes . . . not a few isolated studies of the ridiculous which can hardly be too highly spoken of. The drawback is that they have no more than the faintest connection with the story as such; indeed, it can hardly be said that there is any story in *Marriage*".[11]

Although *Marriage* is not unified by a tight plot line, it moves around recurring themes, situations, and relationships that lend a consistent form to the novel. The first part of *Marriage* satirizes rural Scottish life, the second satirizes English society. In the first part an English beauty visits Scotland, while in the second a rural Scottish lass visits England. In the first part a woman forms a runaway match for love; in the second her daughter marries solely for money. In both sections we are introduced to a succession of unfortunate or failed marriages and to a succession of comic characters—mostly women—whom Ferrier exposes in all their arrogance, vulgarity, stupidity, self-satisfaction, gluttony, or affectation. In each section we are also introduced to a "serious" female character—Mrs. Douglas and then Mary Douglas—who serves to reveal the ideal qualities a woman should possess and the ideal type of marriage into which she should enter. The moral of the novel is clear: women should balance their heads and hearts, marrying neither for passion nor money but entering into a loving relationship approved by both families. Corollary to this is the lesson that a woman who is obedient to her parents, no matter how irrational they may be, and exerts herself successfully in the domestic sphere will find peace and contentment.

The first volume of *Marriage* opens with the classic confrontation of a mercenary father, Lord Courtland, and his daughter, Juliana. The lord, viewing his daughter as part of his worldly goods, assumes she will be willing to cooperate complacently with his desire for further wealth by marrying a decrepit nobleman. Juliana resists her father and runs off with the handsome, good-humored, but indigent Lord Douglas. Like many of the parents and parent-figures in Ferrier's fiction, Lord Courtland is selfish and loveless; but although Juliana is a victim, she is no more sympathetic a character than her father. Her environment, heritage, and education have created a totally self-centered woman devoted to her dogs and her own comfort. As her feelings for young Henry Douglas stem from misinformed romantic notions rather than from real affection, she is unable to deal with the poverty and responsibilities of her marriage. She claims she would follow Henry to a desert, but admits she envisions a desert as "a beautiful place, full of roses and myrtles, and smooth green turf, and murmuring rivulets, and, though very retired, not absolutely out of the world; where one could occasionally see one's friends, and give *dejeunés et fêtes champêtres"* (M, 23).

Following her husband to Scotland, Juliana encounters a true desert in Glenfern Castle where they take shelter with Henry's father and a household of sisters and aunts. Juliana torments her new family with her coterie of lapdogs, macaws, and squirrels, her demand for exotic foods, and her fits of hysterics. She is a comic Mariana in her moated grange, but her mindless selfishness prevents the reader from feeling sorry for her.

The unmarried aunts and sisters of Henry Douglas may be compared to Bella Wilfer's siblings in Charles Dickens's *Our Mutual Friend,* to the party guests in Evelyn Waugh's *Decline and Fall,* or, even more closely perhaps, to the sisters, cousins, and aunts in W. S. Gilbert's *H. M. S. Pinafore:* they have very little individuality, but move as a comic unit—"three long-chinned spinsters . . . [and] five awkward purple girls" (M, 15). These women live far from civilization in a "tall thin gray house, something resembling a tower" (M, 10). They spend their days eating soups made of grease and leeks, sewing unnecessary items, and minding other people's business.

There are few characters with whom one can sympathize in the first part of *Marriage.* The sisters and aunts are complacent in their ignorance, and Henry's father is almost as irascible and unsympathetic as Juliana's parent. Douglas himself, like other men in Ferrier's works, is well-meaning but weak. His love for his wife fades under her willfulness; when he perceives that she does not change after giving birth to twins, he knows the marriage was a sad mistake. He is so undeveloped as a character, however, and so ineffectual, that his tragedy does not touch us.

The only serious, sympathetic character in this first section is Mrs. Douglas, the wife of Henry Douglas's brother, whose sad story was Charlotte Clavering's sole contribution to the text of *Marriage.* Mrs. Douglas is the ideal woman who has, unlike Juliana, forsworn the love of her life to conciliate her family. She has married an unremarkable man with whom she works to create a civilized little paradise from their plot of Scottish wilderness. A loving, unselfish woman, Mrs. Douglas takes on the responsibility of raising Juliana's daughter, Mary, while Juliana returns to London with her long-suffering husband and Mary's twin, Adelaide.

The next few chapters, set in England, trace the final ruin of Juliana's marriage. After wasting what few funds they have, Juliana moves in with her brother. Her husband goes to India. Their daughter Adelaide is raised in the same kind of extravagant, selfish household that formed the character of her mother. Meanwhile, Mary grows up in a pious, simple Scottish household where she comes to resemble her stepmother.

When Mary is full-grown she is sent back to England to meet her true mother and her sister Adelaide, while also being introduced to the new world of English manners and society. Whereas Ferrier satirizes the homeliness and ignorance of Scottish manners and society in the first section, she satirizes the affectation, extravagance, and empty frivolity of English life in the second. Mary meets the gluttonous Dr. Redgill, the haughty Lord Lindore, and a host of comical women with names reminiscent of Restoration comedy: Lady Placid, Mrs. Wiseacre, the Honourable Mrs. Downe Wright, etc. Mary's worldly and humorous cousin, Lady Emily, guides her through the social mazes of London, helping Mary in ways that her selfish mother and twin sister do not.

The conflict of the final section of *Marriage* centers on Mary's ineffectual efforts to establish a loving relationship with her mother, who remains heartless and capricious, and to find the man of her heart. Refusing, like Mrs. Douglas, to marry for money, Mary falls in love with Charles Lennox, the son of a blind woman she has befriended. With some setbacks, Mary and Charles move toward the sort of marriage foreshadowed by that of Mr. and Mrs. Douglas in Scotland. When Juliana will not condone the marriage, Mary refuses to elope as her mother did, although her mother is irrational and capricious. Adelaide, meanwhile, who has married for money rather than love, runs off with the man she thinks she loves, and finds herself a social outcast on the Continent. Only with the proper balance of compatibility, love, and familial approbation, the novel repeatedly assures us, can a woman find happiness in her marriage and usefulness in her life. As the world of the novel is a just one, Juliana finally approves of Mary's engagement before joining her scandalous daughter on the Continent. The novel ends with the marriages of Mary and Charles and of Emily and her Edward. The fortuitous death of Mary's Scottish neighbor, Sir Sampson, provides her and Charles with a fortune on the day of their wedding—a just reward for their virtuous lives and correct decisions. They move away from London to the more healthful and less decadent life of Scotland where, the novel implies, they will pursue lives as worthwhile and meaningful as those of Mr. and Mrs. Douglas.

Humor

Plot summaries do not begin to capture the nature of *Marriage* any more than—though for somewhat different reasons—they capture the essence of *Tristram Shandy*. The plot of Ferrier's work is a slight string holding together the humorous characters and situations in which she delights: "although her books have little *plot*," explains Craik, "they have plenty of events."[12] We remember—not the romance of Mary Douglas and Charles Lennox—but Lady Maclaughlan's penchant for homemade cures, Dr. Redgill's maniacal fascination with food, and Aunt Grizzy's encounter with a ladies' literary group. Craik writes: "Susan Ferrier's greatest power is that of provoking the kind of amusement that vents itself in mirth, and she has that rare power of prodding even the silent solitary student into outright laughter. She has no rigid or limited formula for comedy, but, rather, a wide variety of methods."[13]

The plots of Ferrier's novels are familiar to anyone who has sampled nineteenth-century novels, but her humor is not derivative. It is Scottish, feminine, and uniquely her own. The uncouthness of many of her characters and the relentless manner in which she exposes them are reminiscent of Smollett and Fielding. Her ear for the comedic possibilities of Scottish speech and her eye for clashes between English and Scottish manners rival Scott's. Her ability to create humor from trivial incidents of everyday Scottish life somewhat resembles Galt's. But, while comparisons with these male authors are possible, the perspective and sympathies of her works are intrinsically those of a woman; she is concerned with the lives of women and the spheres in which they move. She is the first woman to create Scottish novels of manners from a woman's point of view and to capture the inherently humorous aspects of Scottish life as a woman perceived them.

The most obvious form of humor in *Marriage* is the profusion of eccentric characters who display their peculiarities in every word they speak. These characters are predictable—only a few characters in Ferrier's fiction are actually surprising—but Ferrier usually maintains a delicate balance to insure that their foibles are not tedious to the reader, no matter how exasperating they may be to the other characters in the fiction. Dr. Redgill, for example, is no more and no less than The Gourmand. His daily feeding is all that concerns him. We come to expect his obsession each time he comes on the scene, but Ferrier's innovation and sense of timing can make us laugh afresh each time, just as we laugh at Lady Teazle or Tabitha Bramble. He is a welcome relief from Mary Douglas's patient suffering in her mother's house and from the incipient sentimentality of her love affair. Even at the culmination of the romantic plot, when Mary is about to leave for her wedding in Scotland, the serious moment is undercut by the good doctor's farewell:

"I wish you a pleasant journey, Miss Mary," cried Dr. Redgill. "The game season is coming on, and—" But the carriage drove off, and the rest of the sentence was dispersed by the wind; and all that could be collected was, "grouse always acceptable—friends at a distance—roebuck stuffed with heather carries well at all times," etc. etc. (*M*, 611–12)

Dr. Redgill and Sir Sampson are exceptional in *Marriage* in that they are comic males who make more than a token appearance. Males do not feature prominently in Ferrier's fiction except in mandatory roles of lover (good or bad) or father-figure (usually negligent). They are there specifically either to help the heroine or to impede her progress toward happiness. Lord Courtland, Lord Lindore, the Laird of Glenfern, the Duke of Altamont, and even Charles Lennox are standard figures from fiction and drama. Ferrier obviously takes only a modicum of interest in them; she is concerned with the lives and characters of women both in her serious plot and in her rich variety of comic scenes.

Sir Sampson affects the fate of Mary Douglas only by dying. Weak of body and mind, dominated by his terrifying wife, Sir Sampson is the comic epitome of the male in *Marriage*. He is introduced in this manner: "The lackey, meanwhile, advanced to the carriage; and, putting in both his hands, as if to catch something, he pulled forth a small bundle, enveloped in a military cloak, the contents of which would have baffled conjecture, but for the large cocked hat and little booted leg which protruded at opposite extremities" (*M*, 56). Sir Sampson is little more than a comic "bundle"—not a real personality. The female characters are the life and focus of the novel.

Marriage purports to be about marriage—the pages are filled with marriages of every description—but it is more accurately concerned with women who are married, women who are considering getting married, and women who have never married. Ferrier presents many of these women as highly absurd and ridiculous creatures, but she also presents serious criticisms of women's personalities and roles. Lady Juliana, as the "heroine" of the first part of the novel, is a prime example of the author's comic strategy: Juliana is an exaggerated character, far too thoughtless and selfish to be realistic. Like Dr. Redgill, she is a "flat" character. But, as the heartless beauty whose upbringing and education have left her without mental resources of any kind, she contributes to a commentary on a very real problem in English society: she reveals both the uselessness of women who are expected only to be beautiful and the resulting deterioration of their characters. Juliana, with her lapdogs and macaws, is comical, especially when we first see her in the primitive castle at Glenfern. But as we see the destruction she wreaks and the merciless manner in which she destroys her husband's love for her, her character assumes a dimension never approached by Dr. Redgill or Sir Sampson.

Ferrier does not allow Juliana to become more than a completely predictable cardboard character, yet, when her follies are piled before us, she becomes less a figure of comedy than one of evil and corruption. In a similar way Dickens moves us from laughing at a character like Mrs. Jellyby to perceiving the tragic results of her actions: Mrs. Jellyby is the same throughout *Bleak House,* but the author manipulates the reader to feel differently about her and to understand her significance more completely as the novel progresses.

Juliana and Adelaide, in their sophistication and heartlessness, are contrasted throughout *Marriage* with the comic aunts and cousins at Glenfern whose errors stem from good-heartedness: though very different, both types of women suffer from the limitations of their education and from the expectations society has of them. The Scottish women, introduced as laughable spinsters, illustrate the smallness of mind that develops in a world where women can do nothing but mend china and sew. These women are more lovable than Juliana and Adelaide, but their lives are equally useless and the possibility of their doing actual harm is very real: Mrs. Douglas must save the baby Mary from their misinformed and potentially lethal ministrations.

The spinsters of Glenfern operate primarily, as mentioned above, as a comic unit. Only Aunt Grizzy becomes an individual for us, separating herself from the others to visit Mary in London, where her simple manners are as out of keeping with the society as Juliana's extravagant humors were in Scotland. Ferrier is again able to manipulate her readers' reactions to a comic character, even though her Grizzy is a fuzzy-headed old woman who reminds us of many other such ladies in British fiction. Her simplicity and gullibility are comic, but the unselfish old woman who sees no harm in anyone stands in contrast to the affectations and cruelty of Juliana and Adelaide. The scene in which Grizzy is virtually robbed by the hypocritical Mrs. Fox, who takes money from her friends under the guise of collecting for charity, is not presented with the slapstick humor of the scenes in Glenfern; we are moved to pity poor Grizzy, even though she is oblivious to the way in which she is exploited.

Thus Grizzy seems to be a fragile character whose innocence prevents her from being pathetic. Yet her good qualities are part of a full spectrum of values on which Ferrier is commenting throughout the novel. Mary, as the ideal heroine, is closer to Grizzy in her simplicity than she is to Juliana and Adelaide; but Mary must balance that simplicity with the good sense, prudence, and experience that Grizzy lacks. Although Grizzy seems, at moments, to emerge from the confines of a one-dimensional comic character, it is her comic role that dominates the novel. Ferrier even awards her the final speech of *Marriage,* countering the serious elements of Sir Sampson's death and Mary's marriage with comedy:

To think of your succeeding to Lady Maclaughlan's laboratory [she says to Mary], all so nicely fitted up with every kind of thing, and especially plenty of the most charming bark, which, I'm sure, will do Colonel Lennox the greatest good, as you know all officers are much the better for bark. I know it was the saving of young Ballingall's life, when he came home in an ague from some place; and I'm certain Lady Maclaughlan will leave you everything that is there, you was always such a favourite. Not but what I must always think that you had a hand in dear Sir Sampson's death. Indeed, I have no doubt of it. Yet at the same time, I don't mean to blame you in the least; for I'm certain, if Sir Sampson had been spared, he would have been delighted, as we all are, at your marriage. (*M,* 615)

Aunt Grizzy and the other women at Glenfern reveal what appear to be the unfortunate results of spinsterhood: an obsessive concern

with trifles, a belief in other people's theories of upbringing and
education, and a tendency to be unworldly about money and people.
As the narrator explains, "Their walk lay amongst threads and
pickles; their sphere extended from the garret to the pantry; and
often as they sought to diverge from it, their instinct always led
them to return to it, as the tract in which they were destined to
move" (M, 231).

Despite the barrenness of the spinsters' lives, however, there are
very few examples in the novel of women whose lives are richer or
happier in the married state: in fact, in their obliviousness, the
ladies of Glenfern are probably happier than any other characters in
Marriage. The marriages of most of the comic characters are funny,
but they reveal the multitudes of ways in which relationships can
fail. Although the affectation of Mrs. Gawffaw and the noisy hilarity
of her husband prevent the reader from sympathizing with them,
we see through them to a disastrous home life, for which each partner
blames the flaws of the other. Lady Sufton lives for show and "proper
pride": having married "Mr. Sufton, a silly old man, who had been
dead to the world for many years" (M, 405), she keeps him in his
chamber until he dies literally and she can give him a splendid
funeral. Mrs. Pullens is the Ultimate Housekeeper whose household
management upsets even the easygoing Mr. Pullens: he can only
comfort himself by thinking that "his lot was the lot of all married
men who are blest with active, managing, economical wives" (M,
543). Unfortunate marriages such as these complement the serious
action of the novel in which Juliana makes the mistake of marrying
poor Henry Douglas and her daughter abandons the Duke of Altamont to run off with Lord Lindore.

Throughout *Marriage* Ferrier relentlessly satirizes the foibles and
flaws of mindless women in both the married and single states.
"There are creatures of the same sort in the male part of the creation,"
the narrator notes at one point, "but it is foreign to my purpose to
describe them at present" (M, 231). Her satire exposes women's
weaknesses, only suggesting the elements of society that helped to
form these weaknesses. Ferrier offers no sympathy. She does not
revile the society that produced the monsters she depicts, but simply
describes a fictional world, much like her own, from which the
reader can draw his or her own conclusions: her social commentaries
are carefully clothed in comedy. She is apt to become homiletic only
on less controversial topics, such as conventional morality and obe-

dience to one's parents. Yet, despite her reluctance to verbalize her social concerns, they permeate the novel. Again and again she turns her humor against women who do not use their minds. Mary Douglas's cousin, Lady Emily, describes them:

Married ladies only celebrated for their good dinners, or their pretty equipages, or their fine jewels. How I should scorn to be talked of as the appendage to any soups or pearls. Then there are the daughters of these ladies—Misses, who are mere misses, and nothing more. Oh! the insipidity of a mere Miss! a soft simpering thing with pink cheeks, and pretty hair, and fashionable clothes;—*sans* eyes for anything but lovers—*sans* ears for anything but flattery—*sans* taste for anything but balls—*sans* brains for anything at all! (*M,* 376–77)

Although Ferrier makes fun of women who do not think, she is also critical of bluestockings and women overly absorbed in intellectualizing. Chapter 64, for example, is an almost self-contained vignette satirizing a women's literary circle, exposing the shallowness of women with literary pretensions. In this chapter may lie another reason for Ferrier's reluctance to admit that she was an author: she despised the smugness and conceit of female critics and writers. These women, in Ferrier's fiction, speak in literary quotations and argue learnedly over the implications of the word *crunch.* In comic opposition to them is poor Aunt Grizzy who understands nothing, including the women's condescension toward her, and only wishes her niece would take part in the poetic conversation: "You used to have the Hermit and all Watts' Hymns by heart, when you was little," she says to Mary (*M,* 556). Mary, as usual, is meant to be the ideal character whose response to literature is intelligent but unaffected: "Mary had been accustomed to read, and to reflect upon what she read, and to apply it to the purpose for which it is valuable, viz. in enlarging her mind and cultivating her taste; but she had never been accustomed to prate, or quote, or sit down for the express purpose of displaying her acquirements" (*M,* 547).

Ferrier was clearly so uncomfortable with the image of the female author that she may well have preferred anonymity to the burden of that identity. Her contempt for "female scribblers" was almost as strong as that of Monk Lewis—but, unlike him, she discriminated between the scribblers and the authors: she does not censure Jane Austen or Maria Edgeworth, but satirizes women such as Mrs. Griffon in *Marriage* who writes the effusive verses of "Billows of

Love." And even more than satirizing the quality of such literary works, Ferrier directs her humor toward the ostentatious manner in which literary authorship is flaunted: it is not surprising that she took refuge in anonymous publication—and never participated in a ladies' literary circle. From a description of the sharp-pointedness of Ferrier's humor, one might assume that she is scornful of women— married or unmarried, homebodies or literary talents: her cruel comedy extends to women of most social strata and dispositions. But her perspectives and sympathies are intrinsically those of a woman; while she is intolerant of women's weaknesses and exploits them to the hilt in her comedy, she exposes and exaggerates flaws common among women in order to contrast them with the virtues and strengths of her serious characters—Mrs. Douglas, Mary, and to a certain extent, Mrs. Lennox. The virtues of these women stand out among the vices and deficiencies of their family and acquaintances—and present a positive balance to the otherwise satiric caricatures of women. Ferrier's major concern is with women and the kinds of existence they have brought on themselves with the assistance, naturally, of men. Like that of many satirists, Ferrier's humor leaves no room for pity; but it is tempered by her efforts to reveal the ideal characteristics women may develop in themselves and the possible ways with which they can deal with the inherent limitations of their lives.

Double Messages in *Marriage*

In a fundamental way Ferrier's first novel is a book for and about women. It depicts elements of Scottish and English life that male writers did not usually describe, and it focuses on females almost to the total exclusion of men. But *Marriage*—and the novels which followed—also express deep-seated and unresolved contradictions not encountered by the majority of male artists. Although Ferrier's creative and comedic powers equalled at times some of the best-known writers of her day, she accepted a conservative, Protestant belief system that led her to doubt the propriety of a woman displaying such powers. Uncomfortable with her own wit and satiric perceptions of society, she sought to whitewash them with moral and sentimental material more "proper" for a woman writer. Her novels read like the collaborative efforts of two unsuited authors— one rather cruel and wickedly funny, the other pious, romantic, and serious.

These two "authors" or voices develop not only contrasting tones, but contradictory themes within the novel. The romantic plot produces the same clichés about honor, obedience, and domestic bliss that are repeated in numerous nineteenth-century novels: if the heroine is virtuous and pious, obeying both her heart and the authority figures in her life, she will eventually attain wealth, a loving husband, and, if particularly lucky, a title. Counterposed to this plot, however, is a wealth of satire and humor that establishes startlingly different themes and appears to undercut the whole fabric of the romantic action. In the satiric elements of the novel we encounter marriages that have failed, households as badly run as any in *Bleak House,* and, most important, women who suffer from their roles in society as daughters, wives, aunts: women who have been badly educated, who have been emotionally and intellectually stunted, who are useless and bored. Again and again Ferrier's comedy exposes the horrors of boredom in the lives of women, be they beautiful socialites or obscure spinsters. But she offers no pity to these women. She does not dilute her satire with pathos, nor does she allow her trapped characters to escape ennui through action as do Charlotte Brontë's Shirley and Elizabeth Gaskell's Margaret Hale.

In Ferrier's fictional scheme the only escape from total boredom is a successful domestic life. Yet, although she sends her young heroine off into married bliss at the end of the novel, she offers almost no scenes, images, or characters indicating that a woman's life *can* become full and significant. A marriage such as Mrs. Douglas's is the best Ferrier can offer: here the woman has accepted with Christian love the necessary compromises in her life. On the one hand, Ferrier offers us—and appears to believe in—the clichés of "living happily ever after"; on the other hand, deeply disconcerted by the realities of women's lives, she exposes those realities through her comedy. Her writing reveals an ongoing argument, a subtle dialogue, that Ferrier herself seems never to have fully recognized.

Of her three novels, *Marriage* expresses this dialogue most forcibly. The simple moral, which Ferrier considered so vital, is deceptive. Interwoven with the serious, pietistic story are hundreds of pages of satiric comedy that reveal the hollowness of the moral. Nancy Paxton examines the language of the serious plot, determining that the heroine, Mary Douglas, has undergone a "radical education" that sets her on a "collision course" with her mother. Paxton claims that in her novels "Susan Ferrier is enjoying a wonderful joke by tricking those 'wise matrons' who unsuspectingly put her apparently conventional 'little volume' into the hands of their innocent daughters."[1] Much of Paxton's analysis does reveal an undercurrent of rebellion against the strictures of society, but there is very little evidence that this undercurrent is at all a conscious one. Ferrier's memoirs, letters, later novels, and even the passages in *Marriage* examined by Paxton expose what might be termed an "unconscious feminism," not a subversive one. Far from being a revolutionary who wanted to subvert the innocent daughters of wise matrons, Ferrier was a pious, politically unenlightened woman who sincerely wished to write a "moral" novel. But, although she developed no radical theories, her novels reveal an inchoate *desire* to rebel. Her feminism is not yet crystallized. Perhaps if she had lived in London or had been born twenty years later, she would have written as directly as Mary Wollstonecraft. Instead, she presents us with comic commentaries through which we can discern her serious, unrealized complaints regarding marriage and the limitations of women's lives.

The first part of *Marriage*, while bringing together the manners of England and Scotland in a confrontation worthy of Scott, also contrasts the situation of married women with that of unmarried ones. The spinsters of Glenfern Castle lead essentially useless lives in an emotionally and intellectually barren environment. Aunt Grizzy and Aunt Jacky sum up the important accomplishments of young ladies in this environment—pieces of needlework: "Most girls of Mary's time of life that ever *I* had anything to do with, had something to show before [Mary's] age. Bella had worked the globe long before she was sixteen; and Baby did her filigree tea-caddy the first quarter she was at Miss Macgowk's. . . ." (*M*, 212).

The narrator summarizes the tasks and virtues of the older women and the young ladies: "to knit stockings, scold servants, cement china, trim bonnets, lecture the poor, and look up to Lady Maclaughlan . . . were the virtues of ripened years and enlarged understandings—what their pupils might hope to arrive at, but could not presume to meddle with. *Their* merits consisted in being compelled to sew certain large portions of white-work; learning to read and write in the worst manner; occasionally *wearing a collar*, and learning the notes on a spinnet" (*M*, 210).

The collar to which the narrator refers is one of the most apt images of the condition of women in this environment. It is a heavy metal contraption designed to improve the female posture: "The collar had long been a galling yoke upon their minds; its iron had entered into their very souls; for it was a collar presented to the family of Glenfern by the wisest, virtuousest, best of women and grandmothers, the good Lady Girnachgowl. . . . Not Venus's girdle even was supposed to confer greater charms than the Girnachgowl collar" (*M*, 213–14).

The men in this novel are in a somewhat better position than the women. The laird has the responsibilities of his cows and lands to distract him; Sir Sampson lives with memories, at least, of his military past; and young Douglas considers becoming a farmer or returning to his military life. These men retain the possibility for action; their lives are not centered on needlework. The manner in which Ferrier presents the men, however, contributes to the theme of protest running persistently through the novel, for, while most of the men are mentally inferior to the women—and some, like Sir Sampson, are physically weaker—they are permitted outlets for their energies that are denied the women. Once again Ferrier offers no overt statement, nor does she offer a solution; she avoids direct confrontation with these controversial problems. She seems to accept the freedom of men and the concomitant boredom of women, be they married or single, as laws of the universe.

It is not possible for either the aunts and "purple" girls in Glenfern or for Lady Juliana in London to escape uselessness and tedium. Due to her selfishness and inability to love, Juliana cannot ease her boredom with the responsibilities of domestic life. Ferrier blames these fundamental aspects of Juliana's character on her education, explaining that she had been "educated for the sole purpose of forming a brilliant establishment, of catching the eye, and captivating the senses" (*M*, 57). But, although not personally guilty of forming her own character, Juliana is nonetheless irredeemable.

Ferrier presents alternatives to these lives of meaningless activity in the noncomic characters of Mrs. Douglas and Mary, Adelaide's twin, whom Juliana has abandoned. Mrs. Douglas spends her life working in concert with her husband, transforming the wilderness into cultivated farmland and raising her niece, Mary. Under the tutelage of her foster mother, Mary gains Mrs. Douglas's inner peace, piety, wisdom, and ability to treat people well despite their faults. As Vineta Colby has pointed out in *Yesterday's Women*, education is a primary factor in Ferrier's theory of character development;[15] because Mary is educated well, she is able to avoid the paralysis experienced by her mother and aunts. Mrs. Douglas believes that uselessness is the primary source of women's disorders, and she educates Mary to be as useful as possible within the limited sphere of women's lives.

Beneath this solution to the overriding problem of the novel, however, runs a thread of irony, or perhaps a doubt that this is, after all, the perfect answer to women's problems. Mrs. Douglas, we see, is not a happy character: she is a strong character who overcomes *un*happiness. Having declined the sort of runaway marriage Juliana makes, she lives with a husband whom she respects but does not passionately love. Her husband, like the other non-comical males of the novel, is unremarkable. From what little we see of him, he obviously lacks his wife's intelligence and sensitivity. Mrs. Douglas's patience and diligence, not her relationship with her husband, prevent her from being as bored as Lady Juliana.

Young Mary's relationship with Charles Lennox in the second part of the novel acquires a balance lacking in that of the Douglases. Mary manages to marry a man she loves and to receive approval from her family. But, although we are assured that Charles is Mary's equal, we see too little of him to assess him closely. He is not introduced until chapter 44, and then he only appears for a few key scenes. As Mary herself is a fairly uninteresting (and sometimes irritating) model heroine and Charles merely the outline of the model male, their marriage seems appropriate. Was Ferrier trying to depict the tedium of a perfect union by boring readers past endurance? It is evident, at any rate, that she did not enter creatively into Charles and Mary's relationship; she relied heavily on the clichés of popular novels of manners. And because their union did not capture her imagination, it does not capture ours.

The oddest aspect of Charles and Mary's relationship is that they are brought together through death. Only with the death of his mother do Charles and Mary recognize their mutual love, joining hands over Mrs. Lennox's corpse. Their wedding day brings yet another death—that of Sir Sampson. He is a comic character whom we can neither pity nor love, so we do not grieve for him. His death, moreover, is necessary to bring the young couple into a fortune. But his death reinforces a somber aspect of their relationship: their wedding is shaded with thoughts of mortality. And, of course, the associations of marriage and death (which are repeated in Lady Sufton's marriage in this novel and in the grotesquely comic

relationship of the peasant couple in *The Inheritance*) contribute to
the psychological, if not symbolic, configuration of the novel. Like
Ferrier's humorous scenes, these deaths illuminate conflicts within
the author.

The relationship between Mary and her cousin Emily reveals even
more clearly than that of Charles and Mary the contradictions in
Ferrier's attitudes toward marriage, the roles of women, and comedy
itself. As the ideal heroine, Mary is characterized by her piety,
docility, and familial affection. Her independent spirit manifests
itself only when her capricious mother forbids her to go to church
and wants her to marry a man she does not love. Emily is of an
altogether different stamp. Lively, witty, contentious, satiric, she
is as independent as Brontë's Shirley and as self-willed as Austen's
Emma. Her humor brightens the last section of the novel. She is
as funny and as cruel as the comic narrator/author—in fact, at times
their voices merge almost completely. Emily takes up quarrels that
Mary will not fight for herself; she exposes the weaknesses of others;
and she deftly creates situations that will bring out the worst qualities of all parties involved. Her long diatribe on the guests expected
at an upcoming ball (chapter 43) is an extended piece of humor as
accurate and cruel as any of the comic narrator's expositions. Emily's
description of Lady Placid, for example, captures the nature of the
woman who manages to turn everything into praise of herself:

"The grossest insult that could be offered she would construe into an
elegant compliment; the very crimes of others she seems to consider as so
much incense offered up at the shrine of her immaculate virtue. I'm certain
she thinks she deserves to be canonised for having kept out of Doctors'
Commons. Never is any affair of that sort alluded to that she does not
cast such a triumphant look towards her husband, as much as to say, 'Here
am I, the paragon of faithful wives and virtuous matrons!' Were I in his
place, I should certainly throw a plate at her head." (*M*, 372)

Despite her prudish nature, Mary laughs at Emily's humor, but
she tries to defend the insufferable characters described by her cousin
with the same argument used by the author to defend Juliana and
Adelaide: they have been badly educated. Emily admits the truth
of this, but offers herself as an example of a woman who has been
able to resist her governesses: ". . . thank heaven! I got the better
of them. *Fascinating* was what they wanted to make me; but whenever the word was mentioned, I used to knit my brows, and frown

upon them in such a sort. The frown, I know, sticks by me; but
no matter—a frowning brow is better than a false heart, and I defy
anyone to say that I am fascinating" (M, 379). Education may be
responsible in large part for the plight of Juliana and Adelaide, just
as it has been a factor in the fate of the aunts and sisters of Glenfern,
but Emily makes it clear that one's character is not entirely in the
hands of one's teachers. Ferrier does not pursue the implicit argument of inherited versus acquired traits which Mary and Emily's
conversation initiates, but the strengths of Emily's viewpoint reveal,
perhaps, the source of the narrator's pitiless attitudes toward the
hapless characters of *Marriage.* Despite her explanations that these
people have been poorly educated, the narrator, like Emily, appears
to condemn the inherent weaknesses that prevent people from escaping the paralysis of their lives.

Emily is the only character in this novel who is funny without
being absurd in herself, the only character whom we laugh with,
not at. She deftly diminishes every type of fashionable woman who
has succumbed to the manners of the day. Her conversational manner
closely resembles Susan Ferrier's private correspondence and reflects
the author's own creed—unspoken, but obvious throughout her
writings:

My perceptions [says Emily] are so peculiarly alive to all that is obnoxious
to them that I could as soon preach my eyes into blindness, or my ears
into deafness, as put down my feelings with chopping logic. If people
will be affected and ridiculous, why must I live in a state of warfare with
myself on account of the feelings they rouse within me? . . . A very saint
must sicken at the sight of affectation, you'll allow. Vulgarity, even innate
vulgarity, is bearable—stupidity itself is pardonable—but affectation is
never to be endured or forgiven. (M, 378–79)

In depicting a character closely resembling her own, Susan Ferrier
creates a complex, intelligent, interesting woman who can stand on
equal footing with any character drawn by the Brontës, Edgeworth,
or Austen. But Ferrier is uncomfortable with Emily. A strong part
of her does not approve of Emily's outspokenness, her satiric wit,
her resistance to society's molds. It is the pious and docile Mary
whom Ferrier puts on a pedestal before her readers. It is Mary who
ostensibly wins, in her mild-mannered way, each small confrontation
with Emily. Emily understands that Mary is a better person than
herself; she praises her friend for possessing qualities the very op-

posite of her own. Mary, she says, "never finds occasion to censure or condemn the conduct of any one, however flagrant it may be in the eyes of others; because she seems to think virtue is better expressed by her own actions than by her neighbours' vices" (*M*, 381). Emily admits that she once thought Mary was an "intellectual ghoul" (*M*, 412), but claims she has since learned that her cousin has a sense of humor—she laughs at her cousin's jokes, even though she does not fabricate them herself. By the end of the novel Emily, like the author, has exalted Mary as the perfect woman of understanding and taste, a blend of womanly patience and docility, obedient to authority figures and able to keep her passions carefully in check. And Mary is rewarded for her virtues by—what else?—a perfect husband.

Emily, too, becomes a wife, but she must accept second-best in a husband. She does, in fact, cast her eye on Mary's lover before she realizes her cousin is interested in him. Emily's betrothed is handsome, brave, charming, but not intelligent or mature. Emily claims that her love for him stems from their early friendship and from the fact that, while he is ignorant, he is unaffected. "I grant you," Emily explains, "Edward talks absurdly, and asks questions *à faire dresser les cheveux* of a Mrs. Bluemits. But that amuses me; for his ignorance is not the ignorance of vulgarity or stupidity, but the ignorance of a light head and a merry heart" (*M*, 584).

Emily is a flawed character who, though perceptive of her own faults, must be discreetly punished for them in a husband who is her inferior. Emily describes Mary's strengths and her own limitations in this way:

Ah! they know little of human nature who think that to perform great actions one must necessarily be a great character. So far from that, I now see there may be much more real greatness of mind displayed in the quiet tenor of a woman's life than in the most brilliant exploits ever performed by man. Methinks I could help to storm a city; but to rule my own spirit is a task beyond me. (*M*, 590)

Emily expresses here the conventional attitude espoused by the serious voice of the novel: her lack of discipline is her fatal flaw which prevents her, in the "just" world of fiction, from attaining the bliss won by the more perfect Mary. Yet, despite the moral implied by the author and by Emily herself, it is apparent that

Emily's lack of discipline is actually an ability to escape the disciplinary bonds imposed by her governesses and other authority figures. It is this same quality that sharpens her vision and wit, enabling her to act as a spokesperson for the author.

Through Emily's humor, which is never far removed from social criticism, Ferrier expresses her complaints more forcibly than anywhere else in the novel. The decorous voice of Susan Ferrier makes it clear that the flaws in Emily's life are due to Emily herself; but the treacherous undertones of the author's voice reveal the real flaws to be in the society that stifles Emily—a society that forces women to wear the Girnachgowl collar. Emily is as out of place in her society as Dorothea Brooke of George Eliot's *Middlemarch* is in hers: "Oh that I had been born the persecuted daughter of some ancient baron bold instead of the spoiled child of a good natured modern earl! Heavens! to think that I must tamely, abjectly submit to be married in the presence of all my family, even in the very parish church! Oh, what detractions from the brilliancy of my star!" (*M,* 591). Her marriage, she states, will be "quite an insipid, every-day affair" (*M,* 590). Lacking George Eliot's vision and more sophisticated perceptions, Ferrier ridicules the limitations of nineteenth-century society and then punishes her character for not conforming to them.

There is nothing in Ferrier's correspondence to indicate that she was aware of incorporating double messages in her writing, or that she consciously experienced the guilt and doubts about herself that she demonstrates through Emily. Ferrier's own education led her to believe that pious docility was admirable in a woman and that even a satiric sense of humor bordered on wickedness. But Ferrier's perceptions were as alive as Emily's to all that was obnoxious to them; she could not hide her complaints about society, nor could she offset the troubling implications of her comedy with a simple moral. She truly wanted to believe that Mary has taken the better part, but she undercut her own arguments with the brilliant character of Emily.

Characters closely resembling Emily do not appear in Ferrier's later novels. As she grew older, Ferrier seems to have disapproved even more strongly of the satiric and rebellious elements in her own personality. She grew more reluctant to verbalize the attitudes Emily upholds. In both *The Inheritance* and *Destiny* the same conflicts within the author remain evident, but they are submerged in more complex plots and more overt moralizing. Gertrude, the heroine of *The Inheritance,* retains some of Emily's independence as well as some of Mary's sweetness and naiveté; but Gertrude must suffer acutely for her flaws before she can win the proper husband: the novel follows a traditional pattern of sin, purgation, and redemption. In *Destiny* Edith suffers greatly from the unkindness of her father, who loves only his male child, and of her betrothed, who she discovers loves another woman. Yet the "sin" for which she must repent is her own despair: her lack of faith and inability to patiently accept the trials of womanhood.

In the more serious atmosphere of these two later novels the uselessness of women and the limitations of their lives remain constant and sometimes bitter themes. As she grew old and nearly blind, Ferrier used her satiric humor to depict characters and situations that would be sources of tragedy for another writer. But she resolutely turned her deepest concerns into comedy and concealed them, even from herself, with comforting plot lines and familiar maxims. Through her strange mixture of comedy and seriousness there may be an unconscious plea for her readers to look more closely at their own lives and the myths they have accepted. Her novels express the confusion experienced by women for centuries as they question, consciously or unconsciously, the patterns imposed on them. Ferrier's biting humor exposes an anger she could not express in any other form.

Chapter Six
The Inheritance

History and Reception

Unfortunately there is no record of Ferrier's creation of *The Inheritance* similar to her correspondence on *Marriage*. She may well have written Charlotte Clavering some details of her second literary effort, but much of the later correspondence between them has been lost or destroyed. Probably the letters would not have given us many insights into the development of the novel, however, as the friendship between the two women had lost much of its intimacy by that time.

We do not even know when Ferrier began to write *The Inheritance*, but she was not ready to sell it until six years after the publication of *Marriage*. She wrote secretly, as before, despite the small size of her family's summer house in Morningside, which was shared with other family members, including her niece Eleanor: "I fear that brat Eleanor may do me some mischief," Ferrier wrote her sister Helen Kinloch; "she is so inquisitive to know what I am writing, and this house is so small, it is very ill-calculated for concealment" (*MC*, 178).

In April, 1823, Ferrier's brother John visited John Murray to discuss publishing *The Inheritance*. Murray was interested before he even saw the manuscript. John Ferrier writes his sister: "He says, if he got a perusal of the MS. or such parts of it as may be written, that he will at once give his proposal of terms. In short, he appears to be *the man*, as he dwelt upon the great talent of the author of 'Marriage' in such a manner as would make me think he will give liberally for its successor" (*MC*, 170).

When Blackwood heard of these preliminary negotiations, however, he entreated Ferrier to give the work to him, claiming it would damage his reputation as a publisher if such a well-known author took her second novel to another publishing house. She refused Blackwood's initial offer of five hundred pounds, but in September, 1823, he paid her "one thousand pounds sterling to be settled for by a bill at twelve months from the date of publication" (*MC*, 171).

In the correspondence following their agreement Blackwood is unceasing in his praise of the new novel:

You have introduced Uncle Adam most happily, and I lost not a moment in sending it to the printers when I had read it. There is a hurried and breathless kind of interest in these last chapters which keeps the mind of the reader in almost as feverish a state as that of your heroine. She is indeed a heroine, and in my humble opinion the only one I recollect of in modern works that one could care much about. (*MC*, 173)

Nothing could be better than the way in which you have managed with Gertrude and Lyndsay, and with Lyndsay and Lewiston particularly. . . . I have not the least doubt of your managing the Colonel with the same tact, and winding the whole story up in a way that will, I am quite confident, place your work along side of those of the author of 'Waverley.' (*MC*, 175)

The novel, published in the spring of 1824, was immediately a success. Ferrier received highly complimentary letters from the friends who were in on her secret. Hannah Mackenzie, the daughter of Henry Mackenzie, wrote her congratulations and recounted the opinions of family and friends who did not know of Ferrier's authorship:

. . . my hearty congratulations on the birth of your second daughter; had I been able I should certainly have come to rejoice over it with you, and to get cake and caudle. Papa is very much pleased with much that he has read (to the end of the second volume), and mama, as is no common case with novels, likes the third greatly the best, thereon I agree with her. Walter Scott dined here one day, and both he and papa joined heartily in their admiration of Uncle Adam and their wish to know who he is. Sir W. also admires Miss Becky Duguid, and said he thought her quite a new character. (*MC*, 186)

Blackwood also wrote to tell Ferrier that Scott had praised the work highly: "he spoke so much *con amore* and entered so completely, and at such a length to me into the spirit of the book and of the characters, that showed me at once the impression it had made on him" (*MC*, 175–76). The Duchess of Argyll, not knowing her friend was an author, wrote engagingly to thank Ferrier for various commissions she had asked her to carry out: "I only hope you will not hate me as much as people generally do those who give them com-

missions, though I was not *quite* as unreasonable as the Lady in
'Inheritance.' Did *you* ever read that book?" (*MC,* 183).

Despite these plaudits, Ferrier remained more concerned with the
secrecy of her authorship than with financial gain and the popularity
of the novel. She writes her sister Helen that she "could not bear
the *fuss* of authorism!" (*MC,* 178). More people guessed her to be
the author of *The Inheritance* than had guessed her to be the author
of *Marriage,* but, like Scott, Ferrier kept her secrets to herself as
much as possible: "All that I require of my friends is to answer
impertinent interrogatories by saying that as *I* don't acknowledge
it, nobody else has a right to say it's mine, that is surely no untruth"
(*MC,* 177–78).

Ferrier's sister Jane Graham wrote her from Stirling Castle on
June 19, 1824, about a conversation that had centered on *The
Inheritance:*

Colonel T. asked me if I h~d seen "The Inheritance," as there was such a
favourable account of it. I said I had. How did I like it? Very much
indeed. Did I know who was the author? No, I do not. Lady A., who
was at the other end of the table, look'd up and gave me such a stare,
but said nothing. . . . Miss Johnstone, who dined here two days since,
told Helen it was in every house in Edinburgh, and the author is as well
known as if the name were prefixed. (*MC,* 181–82)

Soon after its publication, *The Inheritance,* like *Marriage,* was
translated into French (as *L'Heritière*) by the translator of Scott's
novels. The English novelist Catherine Frances Gore was requested
to write a dramatic comedy based on *The Inheritance,* but discovered
that Fitzball had already written one. Gore described Fitzball as
"the distinguished author of the 'Flying Dutchman,'" and sixty other
successful melodramas, represented with great applause at the Sur-
rey, Coburg, City, and Pavilion Theatres, &c. &c—in short, a writer
of very low class" (*MC,* 192). Fitzball's play ran only briefly at
Covent Garden, but its production is, at least, indicative of the
initial popularity of the novel.

Most readers and critics believed that the "Author of *Marriage*"
had grown considerably in her ability to structure a novel and
develop characters. A reviewer for the *Edinburgh Review* wrote: "But
in Miss Ferrier's next novel, 'The Inheritance,' the advance made
in artistic skill and dexterity was remarkable. . . . We are raised

above the petty miseries and *tracasseries* of 'Marriage' into a sphere where higher passions are felt to be at work for higher objects.[1]

Although *Marriage* is consistently funnier and more absurd than *The Inheritance,* the later work retains more characteristics of a well-wrought novel. Oliver Elton writes: *"Marriage* is a *young* book; it is the voice of youth revenging itself on the bores whom it will tolerate if only it may describe them. . . . *The Inheritance* (1824), a much maturer work, is well and carefully built. It shows the powers of Miss Ferrier at their fullest."[2]

Structure

The germ for the plot of Ferrier's second novel came from a famous episode in the Douglas family during the late eighteenth century. The Duchess of Argyll had argued that her son should inherit the Douglas estates, since the heir claimed by the Douglas family was not, she believed, actually the child of the elderly Douglas heiress. Mrs. St. Clair in *The Inheritance* claims the heroine, Gertrude, to be her child, although in fact the girl is the daughter of a lady's maid. At the beginning of the book Mrs. St. Clair, recently widowed, takes her marriageable "daughter" from France to the Scottish home of Gertrude's presumed uncle, Lord Rossville. A proud and petty tyrant, Lord Rossville had been angered by his brother's marriage to Mrs. St. Clair years before and had forced them into genteel poverty on the Continent. Now Mrs. St. Clair hopes to soften his heart with her attractive daughter and her own considerable charms. Her scheme begins to work and Lord Rossville plans that Gertrude will marry his politician nephew, Delmour. Gertrude naturally falls in love with Delmour's younger brother, the self-seeking Colonel Delmour. But it is their cousin, the balanced hero, Edward Lyndsay, who ultimately rescues Gertrude from her errors and wins her heart.

The novel follows the traditional rise-fall-rise pattern of a *Bildungsroman.* Lord Rossville dies before disinheriting Gertrude for disobeying him and preferring Colonel Delmour to his brother. Gertrude, as Lady Rossville, moves to London where, basking in her lover's attentions, she spends extravagantly and lives frivolously, like many misguided heroes and heroines before her. Her fall comes about when a villainous American stranger, Lewiston, begins blackmailing Mrs. St. Clair, announcing he is Gertrude's father, the husband of Mrs. St. Clair's deceased maid. When Gertrude learns this, she throws off all claims as an heiress and dresses in the plain dress of a pauper, like Tennyson's Lady Clare, who is modeled after Gertrude. Meanwhile the unexpected death of the elder Delmour makes Colonel Delmour the new Lord Rossville; unlike Lady Clare's Ronald, he refuses to marry Gertrude as a pauper. She is taken in by her eccentric Uncle Adam, who faithfully loved her grandmother, Lizzie Lundie. Edward Lyndsay remains true to her and eventually she realizes her love for him. In the final happy pages Gertrude becomes mistress of Uncle Adam's estate and Edward Lyndsay inherits Rossville upon the death of Colonel Delmour: Gertrude becomes Lady Rossville once again.

The Inheritance is better plotted than *Marriage,* although, as Craik writes, "any reader can see from a third of the way through, that the charming suitor is no good, and that the virtuous one will win in the end, that the heiress is not who she thinks she is, and that the villainous American, though he may be able to deprive her of a title, will never succeed in establishing himself as her parent."[3] While the plot lacks the mystery and suspense for which Ferrier evidently was striving, the action moves in a more unified direction than in *Marriage*. Characters are explored with more insight and intricacy. The selfish, unloving Mrs. St. Clair is not, like Juliana and Adelaide, a pasteboard character. Gertrude is more complex than her counterpart Mary in *Marriage;* she is ingenuous like Mary, but she is spirited and, like Emily, makes errors for which she must be punished.

The action of *The Inheritance* turns on intricacies of character more than on the melodramatic tricks that seem at first to be the operative machinery. Mrs. St. Clair's skills as an actress and her deep-seated selfishness, which conflict with her glimmerings of affection for Gertrude, establish the action of the novel. Gertrude's passionate nature—which is opposed to her sensitivity, compassion, and intelligence—further entangles the plot. Conflicts between mother and daughter create a more complex dynamic than the relationship between Gertrude and her three suitors. Although the humorous situations and characters are still more memorable than the serious ones, Gertrude and Mrs. St. Clair reveal an important aspect of Ferrier's artistic growth: she learned to depict serious as well as comic personalities and to integrate them with the action of the novel.

Humor

As in *Marriage,* much of the true wealth of *The Inheritance* lies in the comedy. And the comedy, like the major characters, is better integrated into the plot of this second novel: it works with the plot and successfully reinforces the novel's themes and movement. Here Ferrier does not rely simply on humorous caricatures such as Dr. Redgill. Instead, she develops beautifully incongruous situations in which her mismatched characters come to life and blossom. Even some of her humorous characters become rounded, recognizably human figures who surprise us in ways that the comic characters in *Marriage* cannot. The outstanding comic figures, Uncle Adam and Miss Pratt, make the novel worth reading for themselves alone. In them Ferrier reaches the height of her comic art.

Uncle Adam breaks the mold of male characters in Ferrier's work. He does not fit into her standard roles of villain, hero, husband, father, comic foil, or pasteboard caricature. No doubt Uncle Adam comes alive because Ferrier modeled him after her father and after Miss Menie Trotter, just as Emily in *Marriage* is particularly human because she so closely resembles the author herself.

Uncle Adam is a breakthrough in Ferrier's art partly because he is inconsistent, not entirely predictable. A man who has suffered from love, he covers his emotions with irritability and eccentricity: despite his wealth, he lives in a tiny house with no fire and no servant, while letting his estate, Bloom Park, go uninhabited. His latent emotions are stirred only by Gertrude, who strikingly resembles his lost love, Lizzie Lundie. Gertrude's friendship with him leads us to discover the mass of contradictions within him. He despises the "eyes of the world," with which most of the characters in the novel are obsessed, but he is deeply afraid that those prying eyes will think he *does* care for them. He loathes novels, but secretly reads Scott's *Guy Mannering* with delight, hardly able to distinguish its events from real life. He is half-delighted, half-appalled to be reminded of Lizzie Lundie and earnestly fights the softness he perceives in himself.

Much of the humor in Uncle Adam is a result of his being truly a Scotsman: he is one of the few upper-class characters in *The Inheritance* whose personality retains marked Scottish elements. His mixture of frugality, testiness, tenderness, reclusiveness, independence, and dry wit are uniquely Scottish, and his Scottish speech

beautifully reflects his character. Whereas in *Marriage* Ferrier only
uses dialect in a few passages, she shows her true ability in Uncle
Adam's crusty speech.

One of the great comic scenes takes place when Uncle Adam
encounters the peasant wife who treats her husband as though he
is already dead and has prepared his "dead clothes" for him. Uncle
Adam's anger at the preposterous wife builds until he erupts into
a colorful Scottish tirade and throws the dead clothes into the fire.
The subject matter for this comedy is earthier than anything one
encounters in the works of Jane Austen or of most female writers
of the time. By bringing incongruous characters together and carefully timing the inevitable emotional crescendo, Ferrier reveals a
comic sense as sure as that of Chaucer and Charlie Chaplin. Uncle
Adam grows more and more angry at the insensitive wife until he
is goaded into action:

"Airing the honest man's dead-claise when the breath's in his body yet!
Ye're bauld to treat a living man as ye wad a sweel'd corpse, and turn his
very hoose into a kirk-yard! How daur ye set up your face to keep him
frae his ain fireside for ony o' your dead duds?"

And snatching up the paraphernalia so ostentatiously displayed, he
thrust the whole into the fire. "There, that'll gie them a gude toast for
you!" said he, and as they broke into a blaze he quitted the cabin.[4]

Uncle Adam's cranky humor forms a contrast with Miss Pratt's
gossipy, vivacious comedy. Although Miss Pratt is a comic spinster,
she differs considerably from the spinster aunts and sisters in *Marriage*. She has been compared to Miss Bates in *Emma,* but their
spinsterhood is their most common trait. Miss Pratt is an infuri-
ating, insensitive opportunist; only her store of gossip and bright
cheerfulness make her an acceptable guest in the country. She talks
continually of her nephew Anthony Whyte, whom we never meet
but whom we get to know as well as we know Dickens's Mrs. 'Arris.
Ferrier's discourse on Miss Pratt's eyes is one of the best descriptions
in the novel and serves as a good summary of her character:

Her eyes were not by any means fine eyes—they were not reflecting eyes;
they were not soft eyes; they were not sparkling eyes; they were not melting
eyes; they were not penetrating eyes; neither were they restless eyes, nor
rolling eyes, nor squinting eyes, nor prominent eyes—but they were active,
brisk, busy, vigilant, immoveable eyes, that looked as if they could not

be surprised by anything—not even by sleep. They never looked angry or joyous, or perturbed, or melancholy, or heavy; but morning, noon, and night, they shone the same, and conveyed the same impression to the beholder, viz. that they were eyes that had a look—not like the look of Sterne's monk, beyond this world—but a look into all things on the face of this world. (63–64)

The reclusive Uncle Adam would naturally, we assume, be at odds with Miss Pratt: we await their meeting with comic anticipation. But Ferrier disappoints us—and the disappointment is funnier than the scene we had anticipated. To our surprise, Miss Pratt wins his friendship by reading him the stock reports from the newspaper:

Uncle Adam was astonished. He had read of women ascending to the skies in balloons, and descending to the depths of the sea in bells; but for a woman to have entered the *sanctum sanctorum* of the Stock Exchange, and to know to a fraction the difference between 3 per cents red. and 3 per cents acc., and to be mistress of all the dread mysteries of scrip and omnium! it was what Uncle Adam in all his philosophy never had dreamed of, and Miss Pratt rose at least 5 per cent in his estimation. (527)

Miss Pratt's role, as F. R. Hart writes, "is important and individual enough to lift her above the generic level"[5] of a comic busybody. Ferrier surprises us: she does not rely solely on one comic facet of a character as she did in *Marriage*. In *The Inheritance* she establishes comic relationships, dramatic interplay, which she rarely attempted in her first novel.

Miss Pratt is the perfect foil for the tyrannical old Lord Rossville, and Ferrier carries their strained relationship to an unforgettable comic conclusion. Miss Pratt is, of course, a perfect torment for Lord Rossville. She appears when she is least wanted, gossips unashamedly, and embarrasses him in front of his guests: "How do you do, my Lord? no bilious attacks, I hope, of late?—Lady Betty, as stout as ever I see; and my old friend Flora as fat as a collared eel" (60).

The relationship between Miss Pratt and Lord Rossville could be as continuously and repetitiously funny as M'Dow's relationship with Glenroy in *Destiny,* but Ferrier brings it to a comic climax midway through the novel. When the snow prevents her from taking another mode of transportation, Miss Pratt arrives at Rossville in the hearse of a plebeian distiller, "its sable plumes and gilded skulls nodding and grinning in the now livid glimmering of the fast-sinking sun" (476). Lord Rossville is overwhelmed by her audacity and by the symbolism surrounding her arrival. The morning after he is found dead. We do not know if social embarrassment, the chilly night, or his own reflections on death bring him to his end, but it looks very much as though Miss Pratt has triumphed unconsciously and irretrievably. The narrator concludes the chapter in solemn language: "Whence it came, who can tell? Whether from cold, mental disquiet, or irreversible decree? When houre of death is come, let none aske whence nor why!" (485).

As in the scene with Uncle Adam in the cottage, Ferrier turns a potentially serious event into black comedy. The quasi-medieval language of the narrator is counterposed with Lord Rossville's petty nature and the ridiculous cause of his death. Ferrier's timing and her careful balance of the solemn and the absurd create a grotesquely funny scene unsurpassed in her other novels.

Many of the other comic scenes and characters in *The Inheritance* resemble those in *Marriage*. Ferrier refined her satiric tools and employed them with equal success in her second work. Once again she was adept at creating an entire comic unit, the eleven members of the Black family: "fine, stout, blooming, awkward creatures, with shining faces, and straight-combed, though rebellious-looking hair; . . . they all made bows and curtseys, walked with their toes in, stood with their fingers in their mouths—and, in short, were a very fine family" (90). Ferrier continues to dramatize vulgarity and affectation in their funniest forms: the social Bell Black, her sentimental sister Lydia, and the abominable Larkins are predictable but amusing character types. She integrates these characters into the action of the novel and avoids the tedium that can bog down a comedy relying on one-dimensional figures.

The humor of *The Inheritance* is deftly controlled. Miss Pratt and Uncle Adam are somewhat extraneous to the serious plot (although Uncle Adam does provide Gertrude with her second "inheritance"), but both are vital to the thematic concerns of the novel. Like Mrs. St. Clair and Gertrude, Miss Pratt and Uncle Adam attain a dimension that no character but Emily in *Marriage* approaches. In her second work Ferrier uses comic techniques to heighten character rather than simply to designate a stereotype. She develops comic scenes and incongruous couplings, not simply eccentric personalities. Her more extensive use of different types of comic language, including Scottish dialect, reveals a growth in her self-confidence and her capabilities.

In *The Inheritance,* too, Ferrier learned to withdraw her comedy when appropriate. In the final section of the novel she allows serious concerns to dominate without comic distractions; the drama is not totally overshadowed, as it is in *Marriage.* It is this balance that establishes *The Inheritance* as a more mature work than *Marriage.* Lacking the irrepressible humor of the first novel, *The Inheritance* retains a continuity and a central focus that is missing in the extravagant comedy of *Marriage.*

Truth and Dissimulation

Although the plot of *The Inheritance* establishes a unified movement which we do not find in the plot of *Marriage,* the thematic structure contributes significantly to its coherence and continuity. The interplay of thematic concerns is more complex in *The Inheritance* than in the former work: *Marriage* is primarily concerned with the desirable and undesirable elements of male/female relationships and, secondarily, with the relationships between parents and children. The more subtle concerns about the condition of women are, as we have seen, largely unintentional. Ferrier's suppressed anger about the way women are treated and the way they limit their own lives still manifests itself in her second novel, but clearly her vision has become more focused. In her middle age she seems to be less troubled by social inequity, more concerned with mastering her art.

Once again, however, the avowed moral of this novel does not capture the full range of interconnected concerns in this work. In obvious imitation of Jane Austen, Ferrier opens *The Inheritance* with the sentence: "It is a truth, universally acknowledged, that there is no passion so deeply rooted in human nature as that of pride" (1). Other resonances of *Pride and Prejudice* recur throughout *The Inheritance:* Mrs. St. Clair describes the Rossville family as "brimful of pride and prejudice" (11), and Elizabeth Black refers to the "pride and prejudices" of parents (382). Several of the characters in the novel do suffer from excessive self-love—prejudice is less of a major concern—but it could more truly be termed vanity than pride. Lord Rossville's death is due primarily to his punctured vanity; Bell Black's every action is a result of her vanity; Colonel Delmour's love for Gertrude is based more on vanity and love of wealth than feelings for her. Mrs. St. Clair, who sets off the whole action of the novel, acts from complex motives: revenge, frustration, and love of luxury and status as well as a degree of pride. Gertrude, under Delmour's influence, acts foolishly, but her character weakness is not pride or even vanity. Pride, in fact, is not a driving concern of this work, although shades and variants of it affect a number of the characters, and the reader does learn that actions stemming from self-love do not lead to happiness.

A more comprehensive and interesting thematic concern in *The Inheritance* centers on a struggle between truth and dissimulation. Ferrier's interest in true and false identity binds together the plot, the moral issues, and even the humorous aspects of the novel. Gertrude stands at the center of this issue: she is not the person she believes she is. Her whole life is based on false premises: that Mrs. St. Clair is her mother, Lord Rossville her uncle; that she will inherit a fortune; that she is a woman of the "upper class," etc. Yet, paradoxically, she is one of the few characters of the novel who remain true to themselves. She cannot dissimulate: "Mrs. St. Clair had spared no pains to render her daughter as great an adept in dissimulation as she was herself; but all endeavours had proved unsuccessful, and Miss St. Clair remained pretty much as nature had formed her—a mixture of wheat and tares, flowers and weeds" (9).

Gertrude is surrounded by "adepts in dissimulation"; her mother, foremost among them, is a natural actress: "To act a grand and conspicuous part, and regain the station her husband's pusillanimity had lost, was therefore now her sole aim" (9). Colonel Delmour is nearly as successful as Mrs. St. Clair in the part he plays. He hides his selfishness and vanity under a cloak of gallantry and love. He cannot repress his coarseness and intolerance, but Gertrude is blinded by his performance. Lewiston, who represents himself as Gertrude's father, is not as cunning as Mrs. St. Clair. He has no refinements with which to cover himself. His vulgarity and strident manner are the least credible parts of the novel: he is a stock villain. But the very extremity of his behavior is significant, for he sums up the evil implicit in the other characters. He is not more evil than they, simply more blunt. Both through his actions and through his character Lewiston exposes the realities beneath their dissimulation. His crude attempt to appear as Gertrude's father underlines the villainy of Mrs. St. Clair's efforts to appear as her mother. Gertrude's growth is based upon her ability to differentiate truth from falsehood and illusion and to establish her own identity.

The minor as well as the leading characters of *The Inheritance* are separated morally by the truthfulness or falsehood of their self-presentations. Lord Rossville establishes himself as another "false father" to Gertrude and depicts himself as a feudal lord and county leader: the shallowness of his character is exposed continually—and at last fatally—by Miss Pratt. Bell Black longs to be a lady of the county, obviously believing that luxurious surroundings and patronizing behavior will erase her middle-class background. The people with whom Gertrude becomes involved in London exist behind a similar facade of clothes, carriages, and manners. Uncle Adam, Miss Pratt, and Gertrude's cousin Anne Black stand in strong contrast to these characters. They are always unabashedly themselves. Miss Pratt, it is true, is not above a small exaggeration or falsehood to insure herself a dinner invitation, but she, like Uncle Adam, would never alter herself to fit into someone else's mold. Uncle Adam is at constant odds with Bell Black, just as Miss Pratt is with Lord Rossville. Anne Black is clearly meant to be the ideal female figure for whom dissimulation is impossible. Gertrude emulates and learns from her, much as Emily learns from Mary in *Marriage*. And Anne is responsible in large part for Gertrude's "salvation" at the end of the novel.

When Gertrude is untrue to herself due to her infatuation with Colonel Delmour and the obligations she feels to her mother, she is uncomfortable with the people who cannot dissemble. She reneges on her promise to Anne and tries to ignore Edward Lyndsay's unspoken criticisms. Edward never deviates from the truth: he is opposed diametrically to the villains of the novel. From the beginning he attempts to establish a pact of truth with Gertrude: ". . . you say you love truth and sincerity; these are jewels in themselves, and their light may lead even my darkened eyes (as you seem to think them) to discover more. But to drop metaphor, and speak in plain terms—why, since we both profess to like truth, should we not agree to speak it to each other?" (140). Edward also extracts a pledge of truth from Mrs. St. Clair, but she never lives up to her promise.

It is unfortunate that Edward Lyndsay, despite his opposition to Mrs. St. Clair and Colonel Delmour, never wins the reader's heart. He is as bland and dull a hero as Charles Lennox. Ferrier's talents lay in exposing weaknesses, not dramatizing strengths of character. Edward is even more distasteful, perhaps, to some modern readers, as he actively preaches religious doctrine and makes priggish comments such as those in favor of a bowdlerized Shakespeare. His condescending arguments on why Gertrude should love him rather than Colonel Delmour now seem humorous if not actually irritating: "He had not sought [Edward says to himself] to undermine her affections—he had aimed at elevating and ennobling them by extending their sphere beyond the narrow perishable limits of human attachment, and he had hoped that a mind so pure, so lofty, so generous as hers, might yet become enamoured of virtue, might yet be saved from uniting itself with a nature so unworthy of its love" (565).

Lyndsay's efforts to teach Gertrude to attain his own level of perfection make one long for the imperfect hero of *Pride and Prejudice* who learns as much from Elizabeth as she learns from him. But Ferrier did not care for the human foibles depicted in Austen's leading characters. At times verisimilitude is less important to her than moral teaching. We can rejoice that her Christianity was so often overshadowed by her love of unChristian satire and parody: "Perhaps after all," exclaims the narrator of *The Inheritance,* "the only uncloying pleasure in life is that of finding fault" (83). Edward would be more likeable if Ferrier had found a fault in him, but he serves a purpose in his role as polar opposite to those characters representing artifice and dissimulation.

The polarization of truth and dissimulation in *The Inheritance* leads to a flattening of the serious characters: Lewiston, Colonel Delmour, Anne Black, and Edward Lyndsay are figures who could be interchanged with those in dozens of novels. But Gertrude's situation does enable her to alter and grow as her relationships with her lovers and with Mrs. St. Clair undergo changes and tests of various kinds. Gertrude is never in serious moral danger, we feel, but her dilemmas and temptations are more real than those of Mary in *Marriage.* Gertrude, too, is the focus of the reader's attention more than Mary was in the earlier book: this novel is concerned with the development of the heroine more than with a satiric depiction of society.

The two major tests for characters in *The Inheritance* are based on their treatment of difficult acquaintances and their feelings for Scotland. Miss Pratt acts in part as a moral touchstone for the moral values of the other characters: whereas Colonel Delmour, Lord Rossville, and Mrs. St. Clair bait, ignore, or condescend to Miss Pratt, Edward Lyndsay is always kind to her, treating her as he treats everyone.

Scotland is another moral touchstone in the novel. Because Scotland has a less cultured and artificial society than England, Ferrier judged Scottish life to be more conducive to morality and genuine happiness. The rugged landscape and harsh weather added firmness to the Scottish character, and the natural landscapes were appropriate settings for a virtuous domestic life. The innate qualities of a character may be traced in his or her response to Scotland's stern natural beauty. As Vineta Colby writes: "In all three of Susan Ferrier's novels, characters show their real natures—and the quality of their early education—by the way in which they respond to the Scottish landscape."[6] Mrs. St. Clair immediately establishes her moral affinity with Juliana of *Marriage* by her misery in Scottish weather: her unhappiness during the tour of Lord Rossville's estates is very funny to the reader seated warmly indoors. Gertrude, however, comes alive in Scotland:

"Indeed, mamma, I do think there is something fine in such a scene as this, although I can scarcely tell in what the charm exists, or why it should be more deeply felt than scenes of greater beauty and grandeur; but there seems to me something so simple and majestic in such an expanse of mere earth and water, that I feel as if I were looking on nature at the beginning of the creation, when only the sea and the dry land had been formed."

"Rather after the fall, methinks," said Mrs. St. Clair, with a bitter smile, as she drew her cloak round her. (11–12)

Lyndsay brings Gertrude to live in Scotland, whereas Delmour, like Juliana, is happier in London. Other characters, like Bell Black and Lord Rossville, enjoy only the fact that they have a grand house and impressive estates in Scotland; theirs is not the "Wordsworthian fervor" that Colby ascribes to Gertrude.[7]

Ferrier's use of things Scottish as a test of character extends to Scottish music and poetry. True musical and artistic appreciation are guides to moral worth, but those who insist upon their love of foreign arts are apt to be frauds. Lord Rossville, a terrible musician, "affect[s] to despise all music except that of the great composers," choosing to play Beethoven's "Synfonia Pastorale" (51). Miss Pratt's tastes are not refined, but she perceives the absurdity of Lord Rossville's efforts: " 'for I declare Lord Rossville makes a perfect toil of

music . . . Miss St. Clair, my dear, did you ever hear Tibbie
Fowler?' and, in her cracked voice, she struck up that celebrated
ditty" (128–29).

While English culture is less pure and natural than Scottish
culture, that of Europe is corrupt and degenerate. Colonel Delmour
prefers French and Italian songs and poetry. He uses music as a tool
for seduction: ". . . he had hitherto, in the various flirtations in
which he had been engaged, found music a most useful auxiliary,
and by much the safest, as well as the most elegant, medium for
communicating his passion" (130). Like George Eliot's Rosamund,
Colonel Delmour sings with "much taste and expression" (130), but
he does not sing with his soul: music is part of his dissimulation.

Both Gertrude and Anne Black sing Scottish airs rather than
operatic arias. When Gertrude sings "Wilt thou be my dearie,"
Bell and her husband respond characteristically:

"My dearie! what a vulgar expression! How should I look, Major, if you
were to call me your dearie?"
    "Ha! ha! very good; but that is a charming thing you sing, my dear,
'Rosina mia caro,' " said the Major, who was half asleep. (637)

But, while Gertrude sings Scottish airs with feeling, her character
is not yet formed: she obviously concurs with Lyndsay's comments
on the value of Scottish lyrics, but she ends the evening singing
Italian and French duets with Colonel Delmour.

The complexities of Mrs. St. Clair's character are revealed, not
so much through her reactions to Scottish countryside and Scottish
arts, though these are uniformly negative, but through her response
to her childhood home and two remaining sisters. The Black sisters'
house represents Mrs. St. Clair's years of innocence. Her sisters
retain a piety and simplicity which she has lost in her years away
from Scotland. Mrs. St. Clair's return to the house of her birth
brings back natural emotions that have been obscured since her
marriage and life abroad. For the first time she is visibly affected
by her true feelings: "Even the most artificial characters still retain
some natural feelings, and as Mrs. St. Clair crossed the threshold
of her once happy home, and the thoughts of the past rushed over
her, she exclaimed with a burst of anguish, 'Would to God I had
never left it!' and, throwing herself upon a seat, she wept without
control" (98).

Mrs. St. Clair's fondness for her youngest sister, whom she last saw as a child of five and who is now faded and crippled, affects her deeply, as do the relics of a childhood sweetheart whom she deserted to marry an earl's son. These encounters make Mrs. St. Clair sharply aware of the wrong decisions she has made, the life of posturing she has led. In her convulsive sobbing she is a pathetic character. Yet the predominant elements of her character are not altered by this single gush of emotion. One feels that her regret for her deserted lover is based on the same false ideals that caused her to leave him. In marrying St. Clair, "she had dragged out life in exile, poverty, and obscurity; while the one she had forsaken . . . would have led her to the summit of fame, wealth, and honour" (102). Mrs. St. Clair's emotions indicate, too, the fundamental superficiality of her character. She has no reserves of strength from which to draw, but can only cry hysterically. Her sisters' pious calmness cannot touch her. Like Gertrude in her despair at the end of the novel, Mrs. St. Clair finds no strength to deal with true emotions. Unlike Gertrude, she immerses herself in worldly things to stave off her emotions.

This climactic episode in Mrs. St. Clair's life reveals clearly her true feelings for Gertrude as well as for her earlier life. In this moment when she can hide nothing, she turns away from her pretended daughter: "with a look and gesture, expressive only of abhorrence, her mother repelled her from her" (90). Only in artifice can she appear as Gertrude's mother. Gertrude perceives that her mother's treatment of her at this crucial moment is more than her usual caprice and unkindness, and she speaks to Mrs. St. Clair in a manner different from that in which Mary of *Marriage* ever addresses her mother: "I can conceive that you have felt much—but I cannot conceive why—Oh! mamma—what had I done that you should have shook me from you like a venomous reptile?" (105).

At the end of *The Inheritance,* when her shams have been exposed, Mrs. St. Clair retires again to her sisters' house. Here Gertrude comes to offer the forgiveness and solace she has formerly been unable to give her false mother. Her mother has attempted suicide, but she has not emerged from the shadows of death with the peace and knowledge that Gertrude has gained from the ordeal. In fact, rather than remaining with her sisters, Mrs. St. Clair plans to go abroad. She will forsake all the natural pieties of her homeland and return, like Juliana and Adelaide, to what the author implies are the godless, superficial pleasures of the Continent. Mrs. St. Clair's stay in Scotland has not brought her salvation; it has only exposed her corruption.

For Gertrude, Scotland is her homeland and the place that brings her the best and fullest expressions of herself. She encounters the most difficult moral hurdles while in Scotland, but she also finds here her true values, her true family (Uncle Adam), and the man she truly loves. Like more orthodox conversion novels, *The Inheritance* is structured by tests which Gertrude passes or fails. Most of these tests are posed by Colonel Delmour and Mrs. St. Clair, the major forces pulling her away from truth and the virtuous elements of her character. Colonel Delmour plays on her vanity and emotions so that she fails in acts of kindness and in moral judgments. She stops building cottages for the poor on the Rossville estates and turns to extravagant, selfish projects.

Gertrude becomes embarrassed by Miss Pratt and Uncle Adam, even rejoicing when Uncle Adam leaves Rossville: "The seeds of false shame were beginning to be sown in Lady Rossville's heart" (656). Her embarrassment extends to the Black family, whom Edward Lyndsay puts at ease, but to whom Colonel Delmour condescends rudely: "Gertrude felt too much disgusted with the vulgarity and ill-breeding of her relations, to be able to reply; . . . she recoiled from their familiarity with a *hauteur* foreign to her nature" (226).

Little guessing her own humble origins, she agrees with Colonel Delmour's thesis that moral and aesthetic refinement comes with good birth. Delmour claims he could never have loved Uncle Adam's Lizzie Lundie: "Had the huntsman's daughter been an angel and a goddess in one," replied Colonel Delmour warmly, "I could never have thought of her as my wife—there is degradation in the very idea" (78).

Colonel Delmour's steady undermining of Gertrude's fundamental affection and concern for others reaches its climax in London. Away from the benevolent influences of Scotland, Gertrude repeatedly fails the tests confronting her. She buys extravagantly, becomes jealous of the Duchess of St. Ives, repels Lyndsay's concerned interference, and learns the fundamentals of dissimulation. In the scene at the opera, which closely resembles a scene in Fanny Burney's *Evelina*, Gertrude struggles to overcome her vanity, recognizing her own weakness: "How mean—how silly I am!" thought she to herself, "that *dare* not acknowledge my own relations for fear of sharing in the pitiful ridicule of two or three people who are nothing to me!" (703).

Gertrude passes the test at the opera successfully. It occurs, significantly, when Colonel Delmour is elsewhere. But she miserably fails the major test of her London sojourn by reneging on her promise to Anne Black. In not offering William Leslie the living that has become vacant—thus insuring her cousin's marriage to Leslie—she gives in to both her mother's and Colonel Delmour's most selfish demands upon her. Her promise to Anne is kept vicariously by Lyndsay, who finds another living for Leslie; but Gertrude's betrayal brings her into the darkest part of the novel, from which she emerges only in the final pages. F. R. Hart points out that the major weakness in Gertrude's character and, particularly in her relationship with Colonel Delmour, is her "imaginative ardor"[8] and enthusiasm. As Hart argues, she is duped by her idolatry of Delmour—and by her enjoyment of being the "idol of the day" in London. Like Scott, who attributes major historical failures to the enthusiasm of groups such as the Covenanters, Jacobites, and Catholics, Ferrier is wary of excessive passion. Lyndsay's rescue of Gertrude from the raging torrent exemplifies his role in rescuing her from her own torrent of imaginative ardor. Gertrude's spirit, like that of Emily in *Marriage,* must be tamed before she can find her true inheritance. This taming includes the loss of her lover, her mother, her wealth, and even her name. The punishment is very severe for a young woman still in her teens who, far from being dissolute or corrupt, has been misled by her advisors and inflicted with moral burdens beyond the strength of most people her age.

Gertrude even passes through a ritual death before emerging as a new person with a new name, new lover, new family, and new inheritance: first she walks "unconsciously through the valley of the shadow of Death" (879), conquered by a despair she cannot dispel. Her despair is the moral equivalent of her passion through the first part of the novel: "Like all persons of an ardent and enthusiastic temperament," states the narrator, "she flew from one extreme to the other" (879). Her indulgence in grief is similar to her indulgence in love. Only Anne's gentle piety reminds her of the Christian values that bring her spiritual and emotional salvation. She gives up the idolatrous love she held for Colonel Delmour and marries Lyndsay, who offers no sexual or passional threat: "The bewildering glare of romantic passion no longer shed its fair but perishable lustre on the horizon of her existence; but the calm radiance of piety and virtue rose with a steady ray, and brightened the future course of a happy and useful life" (894).

The moral regarding Gertrude's love relationships is very clear. Having worshipped a false idol, she suffers for her error and is finally rewarded for her virtue by marriage to a representative of true values and emotions. The relationship between Gertrude and her mother, however, is more complicated in its moral pattern. As in *Marriage,* Ferrier wavers on parent-child issues, and in this novel her double messages create a moral complexity that cuts across the clear pattern of vice and virtue she is attempting to define.

As in *Marriage,* this murkiness stems from the occasional conflicts of two moral themes: (1) that children should be obedient to their parents and (2) that one should live up to certain high moral standards. In both novels Ferrier confuses her heroines by presenting them with mothers who want them to perform actions the daughters consider immoral. In *Marriage* Mary disobeys Juliana by going to church and by refusing to marry the man her mother has intended for her. She also, however, refuses to marry Lennox without Juliana's approval, despite her mother's obvious arbitrariness and irresponsibility. Luckily, Juliana weakens in her petty vengefulness and gives her consent. Juliana enjoys proprietary rights over Mary, but her span of concentration is that of a child. She is not an actively malignant force. Mary does not become a martyr to parental obedience.

The issue is more serious in *The Inheritance.* Mrs. St. Clair is as vengeful and unloving as Juliana, and her demands on her daughter are far greater. In order for Gertrude to attain maturity and moral excellence, she must face a series of tests in which parental respect and obedience are weighed against her own moral standards. This complex conflict is far more interesting than the standard moral situation of the love triangle. But Ferrier never dares to state outright her real viewpoint on the problem. Once again her concern over complicated issues is at odds with her simplistic moral vision.

Gertrude, as we have seen, is in some ways a combination of Mary and Emily in *Marriage:* she is not a completely meek, mild heroine, although she is not as satiric and self-assured as Emily. She complains to Mrs. St. Clair of the treatment she has received from her, and she establishes a clear identity separate from her mother's. Gertrude reveals her independence, for example, in the opening chapters when she explores Rossville after her first night there, climbing out her uncle's window to explore the grounds. She returns to find her uncle irate, embarrassed that a female should have been seen emerging from his window at that early hour. Lord Rossville expounds at length on feminine impropriety: "certainly nothing, in my opinion, can be more unbecoming, more unfeminine, than to behold a young lady seat herself at the breakfast-table with the complexion of a dairy-maid and the appetite of a ploughman" (40).

In this repressive setting Gertrude suffers the complaint of so many Ferrier women: boredom. Surrounded by people without her sensibility or interests, it is no wonder that she is drawn to the attractive Colonel Delmour, nor is it surprising that she is drawn to him in opposition to her uncle's preference for the older brother.

Lord Rossville wants Gertrude to marry Delmour, and Mrs. St. Clair, to insure Gertrude's inheriting the estate, wants everything that Lord Rossville wants. Gertrude never wavers in her resolute love for Colonel Delmour, and straightforwardly admits it to her mother and uncle. The narrator tells us that Mrs. St. Clair and Lord Rossville exert the wrong kind of authority on Gertrude. We are reminded of the unloving authority inflicted on Susan Ferrier's father by his parents: "So it was with Gertrude; affection would have led her, reason might have guided, but mere authority could never control her" (333). The narrator implies that Gertrude succumbed to disobeying her alleged mother and uncle, not so much by loving Colonel Delmour, but by insisting on it so strongly. Gertrude must be punished eventually for her strength of will.

The model for Gertrude's behavior is found in Anne Black, who quietly suffers her family's prohibition of her marriage to William Leslie. Her letter to Gertrude is a model of Christian piety. She never blames her parents, but simply asks Gertrude to help her overcome the obstacles to her marriage. She makes it clear, too, that her love is not of the uncontrollable, passionate type:

This attachment is no phantom of a heated imagination. Our mutual love is now a principle—it cannot be extinguished, but it may be sacrificed to a still more sacred claim. I again repeat, I never will marry without the consent and blessing of my parents, but were my dear William provided for, I think their pride would yield to their stronger feeling of affection for me. (319)

It is evident that Anne, like Mary in *Marriage,* is to be commended for sacrificing her own interests to those of her parents. Ferrier does not distinguish between the fairly commonsensical Blacks and the completely irresponsible Lady Juliana: parental authority holds sway over daughters wanting to get married.

Ferrier propounds this theory, which is appropriate for the matronly readers who put her novels into their daughters' hands, but then she heightens the complexity of the problem. Anne Black does not have to cope with the irrational behavior of a Lady Juliana or a Mrs. St. Clair. Anne is not banned from attending church, asked to marry someone she dislikes, or ordered to borrow five hundred pounds to pay blackmail demands. She is not, in fact, tested as severely as the heroines of the novels, and we cannot know how pious resignation to her parents' will would withstand such trials.

The scenes in which Mrs. St. Clair demands that Gertrude assist her in paying blackmail to Lewiston are two of Gertrude's most difficult tests, but it is unclear whether her obedience is justified within the moral structure of the novel. Mrs. St. Clair uses filial obedience as a lever for manipulating Gertrude, demanding that Gertrude give all her jewels to Lewiston and then meet him at night in a secluded place. Mrs. St. Clair uses every dramatic device available to get her way, and even manages to make Gertrude ask *her* forgiveness: "I forgive you, Gertrude—I forgive your doubts, your fears, however injurious to me. Go, then; but ere you go, reflect on what you have undertaken—remember you have vowed *unqualified* obedience—there is no middle course" (195).

Gertrude's strong aversion to dissimulation causes her to feel shamed and degraded by the actions her mother forces upon her. Gertrude is afraid of Edward Lyndsay's disapproval and suffers pangs similar to those she experiences when she acts pridefully or disobediently in other situations. Yet, in this novel where moral judgments are continually being pronounced, Ferrier does not clarify whether Gertrude should have resisted her mother, as Mary does in going to church, or acceded to her demands.

The situation concerning William Leslie is far more straightforward. Here Gertrude has promised Anne that she will help Leslie establish himself with a living, but Mrs. St. Clair does not want her niece assisted into such a poor marriage. Once again she exerts mastery over Gertrude:

"But, mamma, I promised—"

"But at present you have no right to perform; you are a minor, you are under pupillage, it is your guardians you must be guided by; wait till you are of age and then do as you think proper. By that time a much better living may be in your gift; for this, I understand, is one of the poorest." (707)

Here Gertrude is also swayed by Colonel Delmour, but her mother's word is very important to her. She gives the living to someone else and then regrets it bitterly: she has clearly failed this test. The only moral we can derive is, not that a young woman should obey her parents, but that she must assess their judgments and decide the validity and morality of each demand they make. Mary in *Marriage,* for example, does go to church against her mother's order, but she obeys her mother's command not to attend the ball. In the moral context of *The Inheritance* Gertrude should realize that her mother's aversion to Colonel Delmour is founded on some valid principles, but that her judgments concerning William Leslie and Lewiston are ill founded. Once again Ferrier presents us with double messages concerning woman's deportment and independence. She would never have stated outright that a young woman should weigh each parental command and decide whether it is proper for her to obey it. But that viewpoint, like her critical commentary on women's lives, is deeply embedded in the moral fabric of the novel.

When Ferrier presents a discussion of parental arrangements of marriages for their daughters, she is careful to put the various viewpoints in the mouths of her characters, so that she herself is not responsible for any of them. Mrs. Black's viewpoint, however, is clearly limited and shallow; Mrs. St. Clair's is domineering and materialistic. Only Miss Elizabeth Black, the proponent of Christian piety, can be viewed as rational and clear-sighted. Her words, however, are the most radical. She disapproves of mothers marrying off their daughters for money when the daughters have no interest in such material goods: "it is surely, therefore, the height of tyranny, to insist upon *their* placing their happiness in the indulgence of those things—upon their sacrificing all their purer, better feelings, to gratify the pride and prejudices of others" (382).

Miss Black's comment, of course, speaks directly to Mrs. Black, who is causing her daughter untold misery by refusing to let her marry William Leslie. Miss Black does amend her statement, however, to refer (unintentionally) to Gertrude's indiscretions as well as, ironically, to the ill-fated marriage of Mrs. St. Clair:

". . . I am far, very far, from upholding those who violate the established orders of society, who fly in the face of parental duty, and sacrifice all that is dear and respectable in feeling to the indulgence of their own selfish passion. On the contrary, I will venture to affirm that connections formed without the consent of parents are so far from being productive of domestic happiness that they are generally marked with disappointment, misfortune, and sorrow." (383)

Miss Elizabeth Black's sensible arguments, like Ferrier's implied moral comments, put the burden of judgment on the daughter as well as the parents. She presents a point of view that perplexes her hearers. While it is not an argument, as Nancy Paxton claims, which approaches that of Mary Wollstonecraft in its revolutionary sentiments, it does reflect Ferrier's concern for the independence and moral decisions of daughters. It also reflects her desire that young women avoid those pitfalls of both marriage and single life that result from domination by parents, family members, and husbands.

As in *Marriage,* there are very few models of an ideal marriage in *The Inheritance.* False parents like Lord Rossville, Mrs. St. Clair, and Lewiston, or limited, vulgar parents like the Blacks, are only interested in marrying their daughters off for money. We must assume that Anne and Gertrude will be models of productive and happy wives, but the novel itself presents only the ennui or mindlessness of women already in the domestic sphere. The only adult women to have attained a degree of happiness are the unmarried Black sisters, who have found peace in their religious lives.

Ferrier, however, is not claiming that the single life is happier than married existence. Many of the unmarried women of the novel suffer from their situations as spinsters. Miss Pratt is clearly a bore, in part because she is single; she is considered eccentric for traveling on her own and ignoring the rules of society which should be keeping her in her place. More acceptable in the eyes of society is poor Miss Becky Duguid, who finds herself at the beck and call of all her selfish family members.

Once again, as in *Marriage,* ennui is the major complaint of single and married women in the novel. The image of Lord Rossville's sister, Lady Betty, with her novel and lapdog, reflects the ultimate uselessness and boredom in a household where women are regarded solely as social instruments for furthering the man's interests. Ferrier does not blame anyone but Lady Betty herself for being dull, but the situation in Rossville Castle allows little else for the lord's unwed sister. Lord Rossville attends to the estate; the elder Delmour is in politics; Colonel Delmour is in the army; Edward Lyndsay is involved in vague business affairs. Gertrude cannot even walk before breakfast. She sighs at the "insipid monotony" of her life at the Misses Blacks' house (357), and is equally bored at Mr. and Mrs. Black's. Despite the superficial resemblances between *The Inheritance* and *Pride and Prejudice,* Gertrude resembles Emma in many ways, suffering from the same enthusiastic impulses and the same frustrations within her limited sphere of action. Only the lessons learned from their mistakes and from their fatherly lovers enable these young women to grow into useful, mature adults.

In this second novel Ferrier's strident satiric voice is muted. She is still concerned, but she no longer seems so outraged, however subliminally, with the condition of nineteenth-century women. More interested in her own art, she created a coherent plot and steered away from digressions such as those in *Marriage:* "doubtless my readers love a well knit story, as much as a well knit stocking," explains the narrator of *The Inheritance,* "and it would be like letting down a stitch to enter upon a long digression at present" (360). As she got older, Ferrier became more interested in moral fiction than in social satire. In *The Inheritance* the learned cleric, Mr. Z—, assures us that the works of immoral and irreligious writers such as Fielding, Smollett, Voltaire, and Rousseau will not be remembered in future generations.

Ferrier was obviously concerned that comedy did not mesh with serious moral intent. Perhaps the very popularity of her first novel prompted her to take the second one more seriously; she glimpsed the real power an author may have. As a result, *The Inheritance* is not as much fun as *Marriage,* nor is it so youthfully critical of society. Ferrier is still confused by her conflicting desires to provide an easy moral for her readers and to express concern for the way women live in a male world. But her major interest lies now in more orthodox moral concerns: the struggle between truth and dissimulation, the evil of vanity. Her primary concern is not that Gertrude establish herself as an independent woman, but that she come into her spiritual as well as her temporal inheritance. These are the concerns that preoccupy Ferrier almost entirely in her third novel. *Destiny* is not the work of a social satirist or a writer of romantic comedy. It is a tragicomedy focused on the relationship between moral vision and fate.

Chapter Seven
Destiny

History and Reception

Destiny was published in 1831, seven years after *The Inheritance*. Once again, we know very little about Ferrier's methods of writing or her reasons for waiting so many years to publish. We do know that she wrote parts of the novel at Stirling Castle, parts at Cathlaw where she was visiting her cousins. Blackwood read sections of the manuscript in August, 1827, but Doyle claims: "[*Destiny*] had not got far in January 1829, when her father died. None of the letters preserved belong to that period or refer to that incident. But no one who has read the correspondence can doubt that the sombre tone which overlays so much of 'Destiny,' the lack of that joyous and boisterous humour which marks Miss Ferrier's earlier work, tells of the shadow of a great loss" (*MC*, 207).

Blackwood wrote a complimentary letter to Ferrier after reading the parts of *Destiny* she had submitted to him. He praised the naturalness of the story and the force of the characters, but criticized the character of the "laird of Inch Oran [sic]," whom he felt had not been successfully developed (*MC*, 209). Ferrier replied with the cryptic sentence: "I am much gratified with your remarks on the MS., and send you the remainder, but at present there is no prospect of my carrying it on" (*MC*, 210).

Later, when the manuscript was finished, Ferrier wrote Blackwood that, as he had told her *The Inheritance* was financially unsuccessful, she would not offer him *Destiny:*

. . . and I certainly never should have thought of *offering* a future work to you after being told the second edition of my former one was 'dead stock' upon your hands. When such was the case I naturally concluded you could not be desirous of entering into a similar speculation, and I was not disposed to press the matter.

Had I been mistaken in my supposition, however, an opportunity was afterwards afforded you by my brother of coming forward if you had any

91

proposals to make; it appeared you had not, and there the matter ends, I hope without offence on either side. I have now only to repeat that I am ready to relieve you of the copyrights of 'Marriage' and 'The Inheritance' at a fair valuation. (*MC*, 214)

Ferrier's brother John acted as her agent, approaching both Blackwood and Cadell, and his negotiations with Cadell were successful. Ferrier's break with Blackwood was furthered also by Walter Scott, who took it upon himself to negotiate with Cadell on the terms for *Destiny*. As a result, *Destiny* was Ferrier's most financially rewarding book: she received £1,700 for it. But the depression of 1825 that had brought financial ruin to Scott was still affecting the publishing trade. On July 21, 1831, John Ferrier wrote his sister that Cadell had

disposed of 2,400 copies of 'Destiny,' and is now, he says, on safe ground. He says the work is well liked and the above is the proof of it. In regard to the copies of the other works, he tells me they are selling fair enough considering, which is all we could expect. He says that the sales are so dull that the publishers in London are resting on their oars, as he himself is doing in regard to Sir Walter's new novel. (*MC*, 224)

For the most part, *Destiny* did not receive the critical acclaim of Ferrier's two earlier works, but the book did delight many of her readers. More people were in on the secret of her authorship, and she received complimentary letters beyond those of her immediate friends and family. Joanna Baillie, the well-known author, wrote a letter of strong praise:

The first volume struck me as extremely clever, the description of the different characters, their dialogues, and the writer's own remarks, excellent. There is a spur both with the writer and the reader on the opening of a work which naturally gives the beginning of a story many advantages; but I must confess your characters never forget their outset, but are well supported to the very end. (*MC*, 227)

Sir James Mackintosh wrote from London that *Destiny* had tempted him away from politics: "On the day of the dissolution of Parliament, and in the critical hours between twelve and three, I was employed in reading part of the second volume of 'Destiny.' My mind was so completely occupied on your colony in Argyllshire that I did not throw away a second thought on kings or parliaments, and was not moved by the general curiosity to stir abroad till I had finished your volume" (*MC,* 228–29).

Mrs. MacDonald Buchanan told Ferrier that her mother and sisters enjoyed *Destiny* thoroughly, although she added jokingly that her sisters were "surprised you could introduce such an unnatural character as Miss Lucy Malcolm, a senseless affected creature pretending to prefer *potatoes* and *milk* to ducks and onions" (*MC,* 221). Most people commented on Ferrier's comedy, but Lady Lilford wrote to a friend that Ferrier's moral views had affected her deeply: "For years, from my earliest youth, I have longed that she should know she was the first human instrument permitted to make a joyous, thoughtless young girl *pause* and reflect" (*MC,* 230). Granville Penn (a descendent of William Penn) commended Ferrier for her "sound and salutary moral," adding that: "We all *doat* [*sic*] on Miss Macaulay, and grieve that she is not living at Richmond or Petersham; and Mr. McDow has supplied me with a new name for our little young dog, whom I have called, in memorial of his little nephew (or niece), Little McFee" (*MC,* 229).

Critics varied considerably in their responses to *Destiny.* Christopher North, in his "Noctes Ambrosianae," praised the character of Molly Macaulay and the scene, which is often condemned for its sentimentality, in which Ronald returns unseen to his home, like Enoch Arden. North also praised Ferrier's dramatization of the Highland character at the beginning of the nineteenth century:

They are the works of a very clever woman, sir, and they have one feature of true and very melancholy interest, quite peculiar to themselves. It is in them alone that the ultimate breaking down and abasement of the Highland character has been depicted. Sir Walter Scott has fixed the enamel of genius over the last fitful gleams of their half-savage chivalry; but a humbler and sadder scene—the age of lucre-banished clans—of chieftains dwindling into imitation-squires—and of chiefs content to barter the recollections of a thousand years for a few gaudy seasons of Almack's and Crockford's—the euthanasia of kilted aldermen and steam-boat *pibrochs* was reserved for Miss Ferrier.[1]

The *Edinburgh Review* declared *Destiny* to be the best of Ferrier's works: "Its framework seems more compact and well ordered than even that of 'Inheritance;' it has equal simplicity with more variety; the story works itself out in natural progression without the aid of mysterious Americans and nocturnal *recontres*."[2] Dedicated to Scott, *Destiny* also received his strong commendation: ". . . by the few, and at the same time the probability, of its incidents, your writings are those of the first person of genius who has disarmed the little pedantry of the Court of Cupid, and of gods and men, and allowed youths and maidens to propose other alliances than those an early choice had pointed out for them" (*MC*, 247).

Other critics, especially in later years, found *Destiny* dull and pietistic. In 1899 a reviewer in *Macmillan's* wrote that *Destiny* "presents the faults of the other novels in an exaggerated form and gives a singularly false and unreal view of life." He commended the characterization of Benbowie and Molly Macaulay, but added that: "The moralisings of the characters whom Miss Ferrier selects for admiration are in this book quite intolerable; and the minister, Mr. McDow, is a caricature so ugly as to be positively offensive, though drawn from a coarse strength."[3]

Saintsbury also finds fault with M'Dow, declaring that he "has the same fault as some of Flaubert's characters—he is too uniformly disgusting."[4] Wendy Craik, however, includes M'Dow in her list of Ferrier's "gallery of superb characters."[5]

Like many novels, *Destiny* received both plaudits and criticism. It did not create the stir of the earlier novels, and many critics believed like Saintsbury, that Ferrier's creative imagination had waned:

She was no longer young [writes Saintsbury]; her stock of originals, taken *sur le vif*, was probably exhausted; her old sarcastic pleasure in cynical delineation was giving way to a somewhat pietistic view of things which is very noticeable in her last novel; and, to crown all, she was in failing health and suffered especially from impaired eyesight.[6]

Destiny would have benefited, no doubt, from the cutting back of some tedious repetition. But the novel does reveal a significant growth in Ferrier's development as an artist. Her sense of character and plot developed steadily in each of her works, although her spontaneity and satiric humor were smothered by her growing seriousness and piety. In *Destiny* the balance between humor and serious narrative, which she had achieved in *The Inheritance*, is gone; *Destiny* is a serious work by an ailing, aging woman who is coming to terms with her religious views and her own mortality. A reader seeking madcap humor will be disappointed. But a patient reader willing to sift through the wheat and the chaff will be well rewarded.

Structure

Like *Marriage, Destiny* opens with a history of an older generation. It focuses only gradually on the children of the laird, Glenroy, and their contemporaries. We are introduced first to the proud, selfish Glenroy, whose first wife dies after producing two children, Norman and Edith. Glenroy marries again, this time taking on an English-woman as selfish as himself, Lady Elizabeth Waldegreave. She and her daughter, Florinda, are similar to Juliana and Adelaide in *Marriage:* mindless ladies interested only in gala parties and magnificent clothes. Lady Elizabeth, however, is a decaying beauty trying vainly to retain her youth. The opening chapters also introduce Reginald, Norman and Edith's cousin, who comes to live with them, and Glenroy's poor relatives, the Malcolms, whose son Ronald plays a major part in *Destiny*.

The marriage of Glenroy and Lady Elizabeth ends in separation: he remains in Scotland and she returns to England with Florinda. Florinda does not appear for several hundred pages after this, but her character and her relationships with the other children fore-shadow her adult character and the relationships that form the drama of the later chapters.

Glenroy is devoted to his son Norman, but his dislike for women extends even to his daughter, Edith. When Norman dies unex-pectedly as a youth, Glenroy transfers all his affection to his nephew, Reginald, and plans the marriage of Reginald and Edith.

Glenroy's two passions are his male heir and his estate. He longs desperately for the one piece of land within his sight that he does not own: Inch Orran. The owner is a crotchety distant relative, similar to Uncle Adam in *The Inheritance* but without Uncle Adam's more endearing characteristics. Inch Orran despises Glenroy's hyp-ocritical efforts to win his affection and wills his estate to young Ronald Malcolm, who is devoted to his family and incapable of petty scheming. Ronald goes to sea and disappears, whereupon his family inherits the rich land. Years later Ronald returns in secret and finds his family apparently happy without him. Fearful of up-setting them by reinstating his claim to the estate, he goes away again.

As the other children grow up, we see that Reginald lacks Ronald's humility and sensitivity. Edith, who has been educated "naturally" by Molly Macaulay, is rooted in the ancient pieties. But her blind love for Reginald is her weakness. Like Gertrude in *The Inheritance,* she idolizes her lover without restraint. When Reginald goes to Europe as a young man, he meets the beautiful Florinda and loves her passionately, a "slave of impulse" as much as Edith is a slave to her abiding affection.

Reginald lacks Edith's emotional honesty as well as her attachment to the bonds of her home and family. While he cannot give up Florinda, he cannot bring himself to tell Edith what has happened. When she does learn of Reginald's passion, she is thrown into despair and, naturally, returns his ring. But Glenroy, in senile decrepitude, does not know the engagement has been called off. He dies, leaving Reginald a fortune.

Edith, now penniless, goes to stay with distant relatives in England where she eventually sees Florinda and Reginald again. Their passion has died, and now they live beyond their means in a loveless marriage. Lady Elizabeth is an old crone whose wearisome vanities foreshadow Florinda's old age. Edith's insight into Reginald's drunken, empty life finishes the cure of her passion for him.

Eventually Edith meets the mysterious Mr. Melcombe and falls in love with him. He is, of course, Ronald Malcolm, who has repented the rashly generous act of his youth and now longs for the love and values of his family. As the story ends, Edith and Ronald come into their inheritance and fulfill their happily wedded destinies.

Humor

An essay on humor in *Destiny,* in the view of most readers, must necessarily be brief. There is no boundless wealth of comedy in Ferrier's last novel. There are, however, significant changes in comic technique: very little of the humor is of a type that one laughs at. In some ways the humor resembles Austen's more reserved, ironic view of personality; there is more wit than satire, more gentle teasing than slapstick.

The minister M'Dow stands out prominently in *Destiny* because he seems to be a vestige from one of the earlier novels. F. R. Hart claims that he is the "closest approximation to satiric caricature" in the novel: "M'Dow is Ferrier's Mr. Collins, yet he is primarily a

ridiculous example of the worldly Scottish minister, from a vulgar
Glasgow background, whose worldliness functions like Miss Pratt's
gossip."[7] Like Dr. Redgill in *Marriage,* M'Dow is uniformly selfish
and insensitive. His lack of religious feeling is an exaggeration of
the ungodliness that Ferrier perceived within some members of the
Scottish ministry. But his vulgarity rather than his worldliness is
the focus of most of the satire. His physical self is the emblem of
the inner man: "His hands and feet were in everybody's way: the
former, indeed, like huge grappling-irons, seized upon everything
they could possibly lay hold of; while the latter were commonly to
be seen sprawling at an immeasurable distance from his body, and
projecting into the very middle of the room, like two prodigious
moles, or bastions."[8] M'Dow's wife and child are equally coarse and
vulgar. Ferrier's description of the baby is as grotesque as any description by Tobias Smollett: "Here Miss M'Dow was disencumbered
of her pelisse and bonnet, and exhibited a coarse, blubber-lipped,
sun-burnt visage, with staring sea-green eyes, a quantity of rough
sandy hair, and mulatto neck, with merely a rim of white above
the shoulders. . . . The gloves were now taken off, and a pair of
thick, mulberry paws set at liberty" (718).

M'Dow's sudden appearance, like Miss Pratt's, often breaks the
seriousness of a scene. There is, in all senses, too much of him, but,
again like Miss Pratt, he points up the absurdity in other characters
and turns sentimental, dramatic, or pious scenes into comedy. His
presence in a scene such as that with Lucy Malcolm and her father
in chapter 18 is a welcome relief from their earnest moralizing.
M'Dow is also a very funny addition to chapter 9, in which Glenroy
and Benbowie visit Inch Orran.

This last scene is a superb piece of comedy reminiscent of *The
Inheritance.* Here Ferrier throws together four eccentric, comic characters—without the stultifying influence of a "serious" character—
and lets them play havoc with one another. Inch Orran enjoys the
discomfort of his guests and feeds an unpalatable dinner to Glenroy
and his gluttonous friend Benbowie. M'Dow unflappably demands
money of everyone and embarrasses Glenroy beyond endurance.
Glenroy is outraged at Inch Orran as well as at M'Dow, but tries
to be charming to his wealthy kinsman. Benbowie attempts to agree
with everyone while trying to swallow his stale bread. The appearance of Inch Orran's vacuous wife compounds the comedy. M'Dow's

huge presence establishes the tone of the whole scene; without him the chapter would be ironic, but with him it is absurdly comic.

M'Dow's appearance in the midst of the dramatic encounter between Florinda and Reginald (chapter 52) functions in another manner. Here, in the only extended scene in which these lovers are alone, Ferrier dramatizes Florinda's skillful manipulations of Reginald, his ambivalent feelings for Edith, and his irrational passion for Florinda. Then M'Dow appears like an avenging spirit: "Suddenly a dark shadow fell upon them, and looking up they perceived (with what feelings may be imagined) the huge person of Mr. M'Dow actually bending over them, with outstretched neck, and eyes and mouth open to their utmost extent" (437). Of course the dark shadow is only a parody of an avenging spirit. He immediately sits next to Florinda and wipes the sweat off his brow with a handkerchief he keeps in his hat. He serves to bring the lovers' encounter to an end before the reader has lost interest. But he is also a vulgar variation of the lovers themselves. When he encounters them, he is on his way to meet his betrothed, Colina Muckle. His worries about Colina's boat trip anticipate and parody Reginald's uncontrollable concern over Florinda on their boat ride. The minister functions here as a reflection of the spiritual emptiness and essential coarseness in Reginald and Florinda which only affectation and training have disguised.

The M'Dow family serves a similar role in London when they visit Reginald and Florinda. Here the parents and children in each family are pitted against each other in a quasi-comic battle of manners, plebeian vulgarity warring with decadent refinement. Yet we see that the interiors of these comically polarized characters are fundamentally the same. They are interested only in gaining and spending and in maintaining their situations in the world—although their respective situations are very different.

M'Dow is an overwhelming character who, rather like Caleb Balderstone in Scott's *The Bride of Lammermoor,* sometimes destroys the balance of the narrative. Like Caleb, however, he also brightens the serious tale. The other "comic" figures in *Destiny* contribute more significantly to the moral messages of the book, but he alone makes us laugh.

Lady Elizabeth, Glenroy's second wife, is reminiscent of Juliana in *Marriage,* and her marriage to a Scottish laird is similar to Juliana's runaway match. But Lady Elizabeth's deterioration into a hideous, selfish crone despised by her daughter and ridiculed by society is not comic. Her desire to appear on Florinda's stage dressed as Venus reflects her moral degeneracy; she is an emblem of the spiritually blind, superficial society around her. Her letter of condolence to Edith on the death of Glenroy, which indicates that she was more overcome by the death of her dog than of her husband, is a bitter piece of satire meant to make us cringe, not laugh.

As in her earlier works, Ferrier employs comic techniques in *Destiny* to reveal affectation and mental vapidity, but her methods and aims are somewhat different here. Benbowie, the ultimate yes-man who is hardly able to function after Glenroy dies, is characterized by a series of hideous waistcoats. Mr. Ribley's mindless joviality and dependence on his wife are summed up in his continual references to "Kitty, my dear." These characters are amusing, but Ferrier does not create absurd, incongruous situations for them, as she does for characters in *The Inheritance,* nor does she elaborate fancifully upon them, as she does in *Marriage.* Instead, these characters move in the background of the work, contributing to the spiritual emptiness surrounding Edith. Their eccentricities are momentarily amusing, but they remain static representations of certain human follies.

Glenroy is the only major figure who retains elements that are both comic and serious. He is similar to Lord Rossville in his insensitivity and pomposity. We enjoy watching him being punctured by Inch Orran and trampled by M'Dow. He is not, however, as exaggerated a caricature as Lord Rossville; Ferrier attempted to create a depth in him that removes him from her group of comic characters. There is a pathetic aspect in Glenroy. We can perceive his pain, as we can perceive Mrs. St. Clair's in *The Inheritance.* But, as with Mrs. St. Clair, the depths of his character do not make us like him more, nor do they make us laugh. His cruel treatment of Edith aligns him closely with Gertrude's false mother, but he lacks her intelligence and momentary self-perceptions. His senility and impotent selfishness, combined with his blind love for Reginald and Norman, make him in some ways a more interesting character than Mrs. St. Clair. His decline after his stroke is a superb picture of a selfish man in his dotage. Like *Destiny* itself, Glenroy's portion of the novel is too long, but it presents nonetheless the most penetrating portrait of a male in Ferrier's work.

In *Destiny* Ferrier employs her comic techniques toward different ends than in her previous novels. She still masterfully dramatizes the eccentricities of personalities, but now she is more interested in a coherent moral vision than in simply poking fun. Rather than dramatizing the potentially humorous scenes between Glenroy and his wife, as she might have in an earlier work, she summarizes them in a few pages. Rather than bringing Glenroy to his death in a few paragraphs, as she does Lord Rossville, she extends his demise for many chapters. Even the potentially comic elements of Glenroy and Molly Macaulay's relationship are left unexplored, and Molly Macaulay is significantly altered from the comic characters of earlier works.

Molly Macaulay is a simple Scotswoman who F. R. Hart claims is related to Lady Maclaughlan of *Marriage* and to Miss Pratt of *The Inheritance*.[9] She is actually more akin to Aunt Grizzy of *Marriage*. Her simplicity and gentle good humor set her apart from the educated and self-assertive Lady Maclaughlan. As a single woman dependent upon the hospitality of others, Molly Macaulay is similar to Miss Pratt, but their personalities and functions within the novels are very different. We should include Molly Macaulay among the comic characters of *Destiny*, but, once again, we rarely laugh at her, as we do at Aunt Grizzy. Mrs. Macaulay is a pious Christian woman whose loyalty to Glenroy, despite his condescending and often cruel treatment, is meant to be a fine element in her character. She holds no grudges, perceives no flaws in anyone. She is as polite to M'Dow and to Inch Orran's wife as to Edith, educating her by natural principles: "Nature spoke wisely [says the narrator] even by the lips of Mrs. Macaulay when she said, 'Childer will be childer, let us do as we will; we cannot put gray heads upon green shoulders!' " (30).

Ferrier's humorous treatment of Molly Macaulay is very gentle. We smile at her simplicity and her continuous ability to see the bright side of things. She is mistreated in many ways, like Becky Duguid of *The Inheritance,* but here Ferrier hardly seems to resent the exploitation. Rather, she lets us enjoy Mrs. Macaulay's simple values, then reminds us that she is an ideal Christian. Like Aunt Grizzy, Molly Macaulay is given the privilege of saying the final words of the novel.

Humor, then, in *Destiny* is modified to fit Ferrier's more serious Christian vision. The doubts that she had while writing *Marriage* concerning the morality of social satire and criticism seem almost

entirely allayed. She has eliminated most of the cruel satire represented by the voice of Emily in *Marriage* and focuses on the docile
Christian voice of Molly. Only in the case of M'Dow does Ferrier's
skill in satiric caricature reassert itself. Presumably she could accept
such satire when it was directed against a corrupt representative of
the church.

And yet, as in the earlier novels, it is the humor that gives life
to *Destiny*. Ferrier's unerring eye for the comic potential in human
nature reinforces her moral concerns while creating scenes and characters that survive the centuries. Without M'Dow's bad jokes, Benbowie's waistcoats, Mr. Ribley's "Kitty, my dear," and the host of
human foibles in *Destiny,* the book would be as difficult to read as
the pious *Life of Howard the Philanthropist* which Ferrier's hero Ronald
praises so vigorously over Pepys's *Memoirs.*

Providential Design

The last of Ferrier's novels is clearly more serious than her earlier
efforts, but paradoxically it is more positive in its message. The
author's Christian beliefs apparently overcame her disgust with the
world; perhaps the illnesses and deaths of her family and friends as
well as her own infirmities made her cling more strongly to the
hope of the Christian message as she grew older. In her last novel
she no longer explodes personality types and social hypocrisy with
her satiric pen, nor is she so concerned with the limitations of
women's roles. There are no Emily figures in *Destiny*. Mrs. Macaulay's calm Christian innocence and Mrs. Malcolm's pious domesticity
make them ideal "mothers" for Edith. Ferrier does not cry out
against the limitations of these women's lives: they are not bored
or useless. The Malcolms, in fact, are the only family in all of
Ferrier's work who can be termed ideal: their happy, united family
stands out against the bleakness of the rest of the novel. Thus in
Destiny domestic joy appears to be a possibility. In *Marriage* and
The Inheritance, despite their comic tone, we can never be sure that
happiness *can* be derived from domesticity.

This novel also, unlike the others, contains an exemplary minister,
Mr. Stuart, the polar extreme of the abominable M'Dow. Ferrier
shows us that true Christian piety, too, is a real possibility. She
does, however, wisely refrain from bringing Mr. Stuart to the fore-
ground of her fictional canvas; she must have realized that virtues

are not as interesting as vices in a novel. But her more positive world view forces her to explore virtue more extensively in *Destiny* than in the earlier works.

Ferrier's optimism here is based on her evident belief that God's ways, though mysterious, are fundamentally fair. In her final speech Molly Macaulay points out "how beautifully it is appointed to us, as to the naatral *{sic}* creation, to have our tribulations and our consolations, if we but look to the hand that sends them!" (835). Looking for consolation in a darkening world, Ferrier rejected skepticism. Her fiction, in which the good are rewarded and the evil punished, becomes a vehicle for expressing her interpretation of the providential design.

The title of the novel reflects Ferrier's belief in a universal plan, the basis for the optimism in the work. But it reflects, too, the unavoidable passing of time, the fate awaiting us all. This theme is repeated in Mrs. Macaulay's frequent remark that things are "sure as death." Ferrier's two other books are only slightly concerned with death: the deaths of Sir Sampson in *Marriage* and Lord Rossville in *The Inheritance* actually provide comedy for the novels. The relationship between marriage and death in *Marriage* is very subtle and probably an unconscious linking on Ferrier's part. *Destiny,* however, is charged with death: Glenroy loses his beloved son and then proceeds to die slowly through many chapters. Edith's mother and Inch Orran die early in the novel, and Ronald Malcolm appears to die. Edith's birth is more akin to a funeral: "A lifeless mother, a widowed father, a funeral procession, tears, regrets, lamentations, and woe— these were the symbols that marked her entrance into life, and cast a gloom upon her infant days" (4). The heroine comes to happiness ultimately through suffering and death-like despair.

The temporariness of human existence in this novel mirrors the passing of a way of life. Dedicated to Scott, *Destiny* deals with some of Scott's major themes: the extinction of the Highland lairds and the growth of a less picturesque, modern society. "Glenroy," writes F. R. Hart, "typifies a late phase in the decadence of the Highland aristocracy."[10] Glenroy is not simply a Highland chief; he is the *last* Highland chief: his heirs will not continue his liberal-handed feudal rule. Like Edgar Ravenswood's father in *The Bride of Lammermoor,* Glenroy passes poverty on to his child. His successor, Reginald, chops down the trees of Glenroy's beloved estate in order to pursue his pleasures in London. Glenroy leaves his daughter to

"Eat the bitter fruits of poverty, humiliation, and dependence" (563). Although her accession to Inch Orran through her marriage finally provides Edith with the rank she deserves, it is clear that Glenroy's funeral is the last gathering of the Highland clans.

Ferrier does not view the passing of the Highland chiefs with Scott's nostalgic regret. She is not interested in ancient customs as he is, nor does she think that Scotland is in imminent danger of being anglicized. Edith's Scotland, unlike Edgar Ravenswood's, is not about to be taken over by English lawyers; rather, it appears to be moving toward democratic independence. Edith's Scotland is still fundamentally rural and morally superior to the materialistic, acquisitive English culture. But it is, nonetheless, in flux, like human life itself, and we cannot direct its course: "We resolve for to-morrow," states the narrator; "to-morrow comes but to root up our resolutions" (248).

The sense of passing time in *Destiny* reflects, of course, Ferrier's increasing age. The death of her father and siblings, and her own failing health, contributed to her heartfelt concern with mutability. A change in focus with regard to her domestic themes also reflects the aging process of the author: now, rather than concentrating on children's responsibilities to their parents, she explores parents' responsibilities to their children.

The heroine of *Destiny* is not faced with excruciating decisions about obedience and loyalty to her parents, as are Mary and Gertrude. Rather, Edith's father and her surrogate parents (Mrs. Macaulay, the Malcolms, Lady Elizabeth, the Ribleys, and the Conways) do or do not live up to the roles they have taken upon themselves. The methods by which the five children in the novel are raised and educated form the basis of their characters. Edith benefits from Mrs. Macaulay's "natural" education, but Reginald and Norman suffer from Glenroy's indulgence. Florinda is ruined by Lady Elizabeth. Ronald Malcolm is formed by the loving family around him; he is the only child in Ferrier's fiction with two loving parents. It is this balanced home life that has provided him with the characteristics Edith lacks—and that she must gain through suffering and a ritual rebirth.

The sufferings Edith must undergo seem out of proportion, however, to her sins. She does not suffer as much as Hardy's Tess or George Eliot's Maggie do for their weaknesses, but she does suffer intensely. Like Gertrude in *The Inheritance*, she goes through a period of sorrow which brings her close to death: "Edith seemed like a bird which had escaped some deadly peril, only to sink down stunned and exhausted, to pant its life away" (479). Ferrier's moral, which foreshadows that of hundreds of Victorian novels, is that a woman's passion must be quenched and replaced by safe, domestic virtues. Edith attains this maturity through pain and forgiveness. Struck down by Reginald's betrayal, her father's death, and the loss of her family home, she begins an upward movement into maturity. She is strengthened by her friends, by her own ability to forgive the wrongs done to her, and by the durability of her childhood ties. She attempts to mend Florinda and Reginald's marriage and to repair the relationship between Florinda and her mother. Her deep-rooted affection for the Malcolms and for Scotland lead her to marriage with Ronald and to the regaining of her wealth and position.

Ferrier makes it clear that Edith's marriage is founded on ancient ties, not on passions. Edith admits to loving Ronald only when she realizes he is her childhood friend. When Ronald finally appears in the last chapter to join his betrothed and his family, Ferrier does not even mention the meeting between him and Edith: she describes only his reunion with his mother and his childhood home.

F. R. Hart compares *Destiny* to Austen's *Persuasion*: "*Destiny*, he writes, "can be seen as a Scottish analogue to *Persuasion*—a romantic analogue, to be sure, and a Christian one."[11] In both novels the heroine waits years for the man of her heart, undergoing a maturing process and entering finally into an intelligent, well-balanced match. But in *Destiny* Edith's Christian awakening is more important than her marriage. We are meant to derive more satisfaction from knowing her soul is saved than from knowing she is well married. There is no fictional salve at the end of the novel claiming that she and Ronald will live happily ever after. Rather, Mrs. Macaulay reminds us that there are no things on earth "that will not for a space of time be joyous, / And for a while be sad and tearful" (836).

In her last novel Ferrier was ultimately concerned with the final destinies of her characters rather than with their earthly goals. As she watched herself and the world she knew aging and dying, she attempted to move her fiction beyond the trivial daily events and the ridiculous human vagaries which entranced her readers in earlier years. Aware, possibly, that her efforts were not entirely successful, she finished the final twenty-three years of her life without publishing any more fiction.

With over a hundred years of hindsight, readers can deplore Ferrier's "misconceptions" about her art. Just as one regrets that Arthur Sullivan preferred writing serious music to operettas, or that Arthur Conan Doyle preferred writing historical novels to detective stories, one may regret that Susan Ferrier wanted to write pious Christian stories rather than social satire. But she must have realized that her efforts to fictionalize the Christian providential design were not as successful as her parodies and satire. Unable to reconcile her comic genius with her moral premises, she gave up writing fiction. At least there is ample reason to rejoice that, prior to ending her career as a novelist, she had plucked Mr. M'Dow and an army of comic eccentrics out of the society around her and captured them for her readers in her three works. Those works insure her place as Scotland's first comic woman novelist—and as one of the funniest writers to emerge from Scotland before the twentieth century.

Chapter Eight
Seeds of Revolution
Problems and Evasions

Susan Ferrier's three novels are remarkable partly because they do not fit easily into the established genres of their time. They are not "silver fork" novels, like those of Lady Charlotte Bury and Catherine Gore, nor are they purely evangelical or regional in their orientation. And they are not simply social satire. With the works of Jane Austen and Maria Edgeworth, Ferrier's three novels transformed, broadened, and elevated the form of the eighteenth-century novel of manners, helping to open the field for the Brontës, Elizabeth Gaskell, George Eliot, Margaret Oliphant, and the whole astonishing range of Victorian women novelists.

It is one of those quirks of historical or literary fate that at the same time in England, Ireland, and Scotland a woman novelist was creating significant works closely attuned to the culture of her respective country. And, although widely different in style and tone, the novels of Austen, Edgeworth, and Ferrier reflect similar concerns, such as education, the boredom of women's lives, and the roles of men and women in society. Similar, too, in some ways is the disparity between the authors' personal lives and the messages dramatized in their books: the three authors—independent, witty, well-read—recommended and dramatized educational and social systems to which they themselves did not conform. Their social satire or protest did not expose explicitly what must have been subconscious or unconscious concerns. While guiding their attractive but not exceptionally talented heroines toward good husbands of rank and fortune, the three authors remained single and privately criticized or poked fun at the social norms that they urged their readers to heed.

These similarities in social perspective did not spring, as they might today, from an exchange of ideas or complaints among the authors in their correspondence with each other or with their women friends. There was as yet no forum for issues related to women and little discussion of women's rights. (Maria Edgeworth did attempt to initiate a woman's journal or paper which would feature the works of prominent women of the day, but the idea never took flight.) Most women authors, despite their own work, assumed that a woman's sphere should be domestic, not intellectual. Mary Wollstonecraft was considered by most to be a fanatic, and yet even she specifically advocated education for women which would assist them in becoming good wives and mothers, not independent working women, unless financial necessity dictated such measures. There was, in fact, almost no occupation open to women above the rank of servant. But in the works of Ferrier and her contemporaries dissent and protest were slowly brewing beneath a seemingly calm acceptance of women's traditional roles.

The Scotland of Susan Ferrier's time provided an oddly fertile ground for the seeds of feminism. Women's education was highly disciplined and strictly limited, but as Edinburgh society was in some ways more relaxed than that of London, Scottish women were more free to act and speak as they pleased. Although they received little or no formal education, many Scottish women pursued their own literary, political, and scientific interests. In this atmosphere of surprising intellectual and social freedom it is disconcerting to find Susan Ferrier, who so much enjoyed intellectual activity herself, poking fun at women whose interests extended beyond the domestic.

But Austen, too, makes fun of or criticizes women who are too literary, while Edgeworth satirizes women with political interests. Louisa Musgrove in *Persuasion* is amusing partly because she turns into a person of "literary taste," and Catherine Morland's reading establishes the comic action of *Northanger Abbey*. Emma has been making lists of books to read since she was a child but has never actually begun reading them; yet this procrastination is presented almost as an endearing flaw in her impulsive nature.

Despite Maria Edgeworth's own independent career and friendship with the brilliant writer and feminist Mary Somerville, Edgeworth's heroines are no more intellectual or independent than Emma. In *Belinda* (1801) she presents us with Mrs. Freke, a horrible, semicomic fanatic (characterized by her name) who fights for women's rights. Her polemical speeches are not meant to be taken seriously. Edgeworth's heroine asserts herself, perhaps, more than Fanny Burney's Evelina or Cecilia; but Belinda is nonetheless educated solely for marriage, as they are.

Consciously or not, Austen, Edgeworth, and Ferrier evaded direct confrontations with the problems facing women who wanted more in their lives than conventional domesticity. The three authors chose to remain unmarried, escaping the tedium of married life but accepting the responsibilities of their parents' households. They scorned the husband-hunting techniques dramatized in fashionable novels, but they did not offer revolutionary alternatives. Instead, they presented subtle, sometimes paradoxical messages on women's roles, focusing principally on what they considered to be the root of the problem: education.

Tentative Solutions

As many critics have pointed out, most of eighteenth- and nineteenth-century fiction centers on education in the broadest sense. *Tom Jones* and *Great Expectations*, *Gulliver's Travels* and *The Ordeal of Richard Feverel* can all be termed novels of education in that the heroes learn truths about the world and about human nature. Women writers, however, tended to be concerned with the education of women, and their novels focus on specific educational issues. The most fashionable novelists were usually traditional and conservative in their views; interested in popular appeal, they adhered closely to what was acceptable to their readers. But the more thoughtful writers began to break the mold that had been established long before the publication of *Evelina*. The works of Ferrier, Austen, and Edgeworth offer both the familiar themes of their fashionable contemporaries and some constructive instruction on overcoming the problems that women faced.

Education was a core issue for British women in the nineteenth century, partly because it was so discriminatory. Middle- and upper-class girls, like Ferrier, were educated in the arts that would help them obtain a husband. Single young ladies played and sang for guests; when girls were married, they gave their place at the pianoforte to those who were as yet unsuccessful in capturing a man's eye. Young ladies also proved their worth by their ability to paint or draw, to produce creditable needlework, and to dance gracefully. When Mr. Rochester asks Jane Eyre to play music and show him her artworks, we can detect a variation of the standard courtship process. Because Jane Eyre has to earn her living, she has been taught more than a woman of fashion, or even a typical middle-class girl. George Eliot's Tom Tulliver is taught algebra and Latin, though he has little aptitude for such studies, and his sister Maggie is left to read whatever she can find.

Susan Ferrier's letters and novels reveal the tedium of such an intellectually restricted life. Her description of the Girnachgowl collar in *Marriage* is not a comic extravagance; it is a very real image of the contraptions girls were forced to wear and a vivid metaphor for their education and their lives. The intermittent boredom of her three heroines reflects what was clearly a personal problem for her: Mary is trapped in Juliana's fashionable household; Gertrude suffers the boredom of Rossville; Edith is bored and useless at the Ribleys'. At moments we are even sympathetic to Juliana's plight at Glenfern. Like Austen's Emma, these women have no suitable outlets for their energies and their intelligence.

Despite their understanding of the dilemmas of the women around them, Ferrier, Austen, and Edgeworth propose a fairly standard solution: educate a woman's emotions properly, they claim, and she will become a worthwhile person. It is not what women study but the qualities of their teachers that affect their lives most profoundly; their teachers can help them survive the boredom of their later lives. For this purpose, the parent is presented as the best possible teacher. The authors do not advocate sending girls to school. Both Ferrier and Edgeworth were influenced by Anna Laetitia Barbauld's (1743–1825) essay "On Education," which states that parents should not despair if their children do not learn great quantities of facts: "Are children then to be neglected? Surely not: but having given them the instruction and accomplishments which their situation in life requires, let us reject superfluous solicitude and trust that their characters will form themselves from the spontaneous influence of good examples, and circumstances which impel them to useful action."[1] Barbauld refused to take part in founding a "Ladies' College," maintaining that learning outside of certain prescribed spheres prevents a woman from becoming a good wife or companion. Conversation with a husband or father, she asserted, was more worthwhile than a school education.

This dictum was easily applied to women by many nineteenth-century educational theorists as it was believed that women were composed of more emotion than intellect. Their passions must be tamed by their educational processes; a deficient parent could be a woman's ruin. In Edgeworth's *Patronage* the beautiful Miss Hauton

is found to be the daughter of a remarried divorcée. This is cause
enough for some people to shun her, but the worthy Mrs. Percy
states that judgment should be based on the young lady's exposure
to her erring mother: "[Mrs. Percy] said that she thought the important point to be considered was, what the *education* of the daughter
had been; on this a prudent man would form his opinion, not on
the mere accident of birth. He would inquire whether the girl had
lived with the ill-conducted mother—had been in situations to be
influenced by the company which she kept. If such had been the
case, Mrs. Percy declared she thought it would be imprudent and
wrong to marry the daughter."[2] The unfortunate Miss Hauton, it
turns out, *has* been contaminated by her mother and, though she
struggles to act rightly, her poor education proves too much for
her.

Fashionable Scottish literature of this period is filled with young
ladies who suffer fatally from an excess of passion or who valiantly
conquer it. Almost always, education determines their success or
failure. Ferrier's friend Lady Charlotte Bury presents us with an
orphaned heroine in *Conduct is Fate* (1822). Raised by her aunts,
Bertha "received little or nothing of what is termed education. . . .
[Her] reading was of that desultory kind which raised the mind to
soar in a vague sublime, but in nowise chastises the imagination,
or forms the judgment to the sober relish of real life."[3] In a thoughtless moment Bertha gives in to a clandestine marriage which leads
her through three torturous volumes filled with her repentance and
misery, but larded with exotic intrigue, hidden identities, and the
other ingredients of romance. Because she is basically good at heart,
Bertha is saved from a totally tragic end; Bury relegates her simply
to widowhood made tolerable by the strength of her Christian beliefs.

Mary Brunton's Scottish heroine Laura in *Self-Control* (1811) is a
more admirable young woman than Bertha. Despite the early death
of her mother, Laura is educated quite well by her father. She
succumbs, however, to a brief (and innocent) passion for the villainous Harville which she must overcome and for which she must
suffer. After her father's death she is surrounded by temptations
that might ruin any young girl less controlled than Laura, but the
education provided by her father keeps her strong and virtuous.

Examples of this dominant theme in early nineteenth-century
novels could go on almost endlessly: Elizabeth Hamilton's Miss
Stewart in *The Cottagers of Glenburnie* makes a near-calamitous match

because her father has been too lenient in her education; Mrs. McLarty's children all suffer because she "canna be fash'd" with them. English novels reflect the same point of view: Lydia Bennet's elopement in *Pride and Prejudice* is a tragic result of her father's laziness. Emma's education is completed by her father-figure lover, as Mr. Woodhouse cannot provide the control and education she needs.

Ferrier's concern, then, with parents (and parent-figures) and the education of their daughters is similar to that of many women writers of her time. Her picture of the twins—Adelaide ruined by her mother while Mary is redeemed by her foster-mother—is a perfect paradigm of nineteenth-century educational theory. Heredity does not matter very much: Mary Douglas resembles only her aunt by marriage and bears no resemblance to her own mother and twin sister. Edith in *Destiny* is saved by the "natural" education of Mrs. Macaulay, inheriting none of her father's weaknesses. *The Inheritance* presents a somewhat different situation, as Gertrude is almost grown up when we meet her. But she has successfully resisted Mrs. St. Clair's attempts to teach her artful manners, probably because she was taught in part by her good nurse who really was her mother. Without a good parent's assistance as a young woman, however, Gertrude fails to make proper and discerning decisions; like Emma, she attains her final education into adulthood partially through the wisdom of her lover.

In Ferrier's novels the heroines are educated to control their passions and to maintain *good taste*. They may not be knowledgeable about art or poetry, but they know enough to discern affectation. They favor native ballads over opera, wild country landscapes over cultivated gardens, and natural emotions over highly mannered expression. They learn to be kind to the poor, rude, and vulgar. They choose finally to live a retired domestic life in Scotland rather than a brilliant social life in England. They have all learned enough to make discerning comments about the impropriety of reading Byron and Fielding and the advantages of studying more uplifting literature, but they do not take part in literary discussions: such conversation would indicate a forwardness and masculine intelligence inappropriate to a young lady. The values for a woman's behavior incorporated into Ferrier's works are similar to those in countless novels by male authors: Scott's Edward Waverley falls in love with the highly educated Flora, but he marries the innocent Rose, who asks him to help her with her reading.

Ferrier accepts the traditional viewpoint that too much education or even, simply, assertiveness can be damaging to a woman, as it is to Lady Emily in *Marriage*. As we have seen, however, Ferrier does advocate more independence in her heroines than Fanny Burney did in hers. Mary Douglas rightfully resists her mother on occasion; Gertrude is actually wrong to give in to her mother on certain points. The heroines should receive familial approval before marrying, but clearly the young women should develop their own value systems independent of their parents. Similarly, Anne Elliot must learn firmness in *Persuasion*. The heroine of Edgeworth's *Emilie de Coulanges* remains independent of her mother-figure, Mrs. Somers. Modern readers may find it annoying that Edgeworth's Clarence Hervey is permitted to "test" Belinda's worthiness (i.e., education), much as Lord Orville tests Evelina's. But Belinda does not give in entirely to her matchmaking aunt and Mrs. Stanhope. The heroines of these nineteenth-century novels are not obvious predecessors of the twentieth-century woman, but they have clearly advanced from Evelina and Julia de Roubigné.

Ferrier, Austen, and Edgeworth may have avoided dramatizing the problems of the artistic or intellectual woman partly because they considered themselves to be exceptional; perhaps they felt that fictional characters similar to themselves would be of no interest to their readers. Anna Laetitia Barbauld writes to that effect: "Perhaps you may think that having myself stepped out of the bounds of female reserve in becoming an author it is with an ill grace that I offer these sentiments [discouraging female education in a college]— but my situation has been peculiar and would be no rule for others."[4] Maria Edgeworth, an educational theorist who co-authored *Practical Education* with her father and produced extremely popular educational children's stories, was as conservative as the more retiring Austen and Ferrier. These writers, like Barbauld, tailored their views to the "average" woman interested only in marriage and motherhood. The flaws in their depictions of domestic bliss lie in the singularly vivid representations of the boredom and unpleasantness of women's lives.

A close look at the marriages surrounding Mary, Gertrude, and Edith—as well as Belinda, Emilie, Emma, Anne, and the other heroines of these novels—leaves us little hope that marriage can bring much more than ennui and frustration to a woman. The authors present only limited solutions to these problems: discipline one's emotions, accept one's role, marry properly—and teach one's daughters to do the same. The possibility that a woman could find satisfaction in scholarly or artistic pursuits is never developed. George Eliot's presentation in 1876 of Daniel Deronda's unmotherly but artistically successful mother is one of the first portraits of a woman artist. Yet one cannot say that even here the author dramatically explores her situation and character.

Virginia Woolf's Lily Briscoe in *To The Lighthouse* (1927) provides an apt image for the woman artist prior to very recent decades. Like Ferrier and her contemporaries, Lily works alone amid the seemingly more useful domestic activities around her. She is frustrated, aware of her limitations, but dedicated—and she hardly knows why she is any of these things. Lily, at least, is finally awarded a partial revelation of her own function and worth as a woman and artist. Ferrier, in the little we can glean from her novels and letters, was never granted such illumination.

Nineteenth-century woman artists and intellectuals were lonely figures. They had few models to emulate, and they found little solace for their situation in religion or philosophy. It is no wonder that, rather than create fictional characters like themselves, they proffered contradictory "solutions" to their own dilemmas. Susan Ferrier probably did not analyze her paradoxical nature; she simply attempted to punish her rebellious self in her novels and then attempted to overcome it completely in her later years.

Chapter 9

Susan Ferrier
and the Scottish Novel

Flowering

In the previous chapter we saw some of the characteristic problems and themes that bind Ferrier's works to those of other women writers of her time. Now, in this final chapter, we must view her work in terms of Scottish fiction, for the texture and content of her novels are inextricably bound to the place and time in which she lived. Moreover, the sudden rise and subsequent decline in popularity of her works are closely related to the history of Scottish fiction in the nineteenth century.

The novel form emerged spectacularly in Scotland in the first part of the nineteenth century, long after it had been established in England. There is no adequate explanation for this sudden flowering. It is a literary phenomenon that cannot be explained totally in rational terms: through coincidence and luck, a number of talented writers flourished within a small geographical area for less than a century and produced a remarkable collection of novels.

Part of the explanation is undoubtedly political and economic. The peace of the Union with England in 1707 improved the Scottish economy and allowed Scottish writers more time for literary work. But the Union also caused much of the emotional tension that found a voice in fiction. F. R. Hart writes that "by ending political independence the Union had forced Scotland into greater cultural consciousness, awakened a defensive pride, and led to a revival of interest in her literary nationality."[1] Fears that Scotland would lose its cultural identity and native speech—and that it would succumb to the moral evils of a corrupt English society—are implicit throughout the pages of Scottish fiction. Affection for Scottish landscape, Scottish history, and the foibles of Scottish character are mainstays of these novels. Characters who prefer English manners to Scottish in Ferrier's books, for example, are apt to be morally irresponsible or even inherently evil. There is hardly a European or American in the works of Susan Ferrier, John Galt, or Walter Scott who is not a villain or, at best, a figure of fun.

Fundamental to this fierce nationalism in post-Union Scotland were conflicting emotions about Scottish religion. Religion had torn Scotland apart for centuries and even in the calm of nineteenth-century English tolerance it pervaded the souls of Scottish writers. It appears explicitly in the historical fiction of Scott and the satire of James Hogg; it permeates the consciousness of Lockhart and Galt. In Ferrier it led to self-doubts which affected her creative energies and eventually helped stop their flow. Calvinist disapproval of "profane" literature influenced even the most enlightened nineteenth-century writers. Fiction was closely associated with lying and was thus considered sinful. In order to gain approval for his *Annals of the Parish* Galt disguised it as autobiography. The urbane and cultured Scott wrote novel after novel anonymously, claiming it would be improper for a Clerk of Session to write fiction. Ferrier's heroes and heroines would never read Smollett or Fielding, and they highly recommend reading only a bowdlerized Shakespeare. Ferrier herself felt increasingly guilty about producing profane literature and endeavored to compensate for her frivolity with increased doses of pious reflection in her works. Deep-seated religious beliefs such as these undoubtedly contributed to the slow emergence of the Scottish novel in the late eighteenth century. Then, when Scottish fiction did begin to appear, religion was a dominant motif, as were concomitant themes of guilt, penance, and retribution.

Like Scottish religion, Scottish language was a major force which both inhibited the growth of the Scottish novel and affected it deeply. The Scottish people fostered a chronic language problem, speaking their own highly individualistic Scots while attempting to write traditional English prose. Lacking the idiomatic usage that comes from writing a language one speaks, Scottish anglicized prose suffered from a lack of animation and innovativeness. Only when nationalistic fervor, coupled with the success of Burns's poems and Scott's ballad-gathering, legitimized the use of dialect did Scottish writing begin to take a natural, individualized form.

Scottish novelists, however, tended to reconcile their love of dialect with their belief that "proper" literature should be written in standard English by creating servants, peasants, and comic figures who speak dialect while the upper-class heroes and heroines speak

English. The result of this compromise is that the refined figures
in the novels rarely seem real. Scott's Jeanie Deans is a real person,
but Edward Waverley is a stick. Ferrier's wonderful Scots dialect
pours out of Uncle Adam in *The Inheritance,* but Gertrude's speech
never comes alive. Galt's genius lies partly in his ability to maintain
powerful Scottish speech through entire novels: the irrepressible
narrator of *The Provost* could never be captured in English prose. If
the Union of 1707 had not heightened the Scots' delight in their
native tongue, writers might have continued to create only tepid
imitations of English works. At the same time, continuing ambivalence about their speech created major artistic problems in many
of their novels.

The tensions and confusion brought about by the Union of 1707
affected the attitudes of Scottish writers toward not only language,
but religion, society, and art itself. Scott's epic views of the historical
struggles between Scotland and England in the best of his novels
grew out of this tension, as did Galt's close examinations of changing
life in Scottish communities and Ferrier's depictions of the differences between English and Scottish manners. But, of course, the
sudden emergence of an art form is never a purely historical phenomenon. The novels of Susan Ferrier and her contemporaries are
rooted in literary traditions and were influenced by a wide range of
factors.

Ferrier's works stem basically from three distinct literary modes:
she is a novelist of manners who write tales similar to Fanny Burney's
Evelina, but she is also a Scottish regionalist, like Scott, who captured elements of Scottish life and character. Her works also reflect
the influence of her friend Henry Mackenzie, the Scottish novelist
of sentiment, whose works sprang principally from English traditions: Mackenzie reminded English readers of Laurence Sterne and
Samuel Richardson. *The Man of Feeling* and *Julia de Roubigné* appealed
to the late eighteenth-century audience's taste for sensibility and
heartfelt feeling. Mackenzie was acceptable to the English audience
also because he did not emphasize a Scottish background in his
books, nor did he use Scots dialect. For the most part his novels
were "Scottish" simply because their author lived in Edinburgh.

Like Scott in later years, however, Mackenzie was read by all the
Scottish novelists of the nineteenth century, and his influence is
pervasive. The fundamental tragic tone in his works, which F. R.
Hart describes as "the grimmest sort of ballad-like intensity, tragic

irony, sudden violence,"[2] is echoed in many Scottish novels of the following century, including *The Bride of Lammermoor*. The tone stems, perhaps, from the same elements of Scottish character that produced the ballad of "The Twa Corbies" and the peculiarly grim aspects of Scottish religion, but Mackenzie was the first to use it successfully in novels.

Ferrier employed a tragic tone similar to Mackenzie's at climactic moments in her works, particularly in *Destiny*, but she was more attracted to the sentimental aspects of Mackenzie's fiction. She did not cause her sentimental heroines to suffer as intensely as Julia de Roubigné: Mary, Edith, and Gertrude are each saved from ultimate disaster. But her heroines retain a sensibility similar to Julia's. They are *capable* of suffering. Ferrier's sensitive heroes, like Mackenzie's Man of Feeling, do not hesitate to cry. Her major characters, like Mackenzie's, are involved in moral and emotional struggles that separate them in some measure from a specific historical time frame or regional locale.

Ferrier's heroines retain few particularly Scottish characteristics and encounter problems familiar to hundreds of non-Scottish nineteenth-century heroines, but most of her minor characters are clearly and uniquely Scottish. Scotland is itself almost a character in these volumes: Scottish art and music embody aesthetic and moral values; Scottish weather builds character; Scottish scenery is stark but splendid; Scottish culture is provincial, but not decadent like that of England.

Ferrier's focus on Scotland and Scottish character and manners stemmed more or less directly from the influence of Walter Scott. His poems and novels catapulted Scotland into the limelight all over the world, making Scottish characteristics popular and respectable subjects for poetry and fiction. In Scotland itself Scott actually made the novel form respectable.

There is no evidence that Ferrier resented Scott's success. She was not a jealous writer. But his novels put hers—and those of all his Scottish contemporaries—in the shade. Ironically, they also contributed to the success of her works. As a result of the Waverley Novels, the Scottish novel was a fad in Europe and America for nearly half a century and permanently affected the country as a whole. Craig writes: "*St. Ronan's Well* by itself turned the little country place in which it was set, Innerleithen, into a crowded, highly successful Border resort; and the boom in tartan-making

stimulated by the Waverley Novels contributed to the growth of
Stirling between 1821 and 1841."[3] Scott's influence was "in the
wind" and clearly affected Ferrier's literary efforts. Largely because
of him, as Kurt Wittig writes, "The Scottish background was now
ripe for exploitation."[4]

Ferrier dramatizes idiosyncrasies of Scottish character, as does
Scott, and juxtaposes the cultural differences between England and
Scotland for serious and comedic purposes. Like Scott, too, she deftly
uses Scottish dialect for her peasant and comic characters, and describes Scottish manners and ways of life. She does not have Scott's
historical vision, but she captures insights into the details of every-
day life that he rarely touches. Scott wrote in his diary that "Edgeworth, Ferrier, Austen, have all given portraits of real society, far
superior to anything man, vain man, has produced of the like nature."[5]

Scott himself is epic in his scope; Ferrier captures mundane minu-
tiae, primarily for comic effect. She is conscious, particularly in
Destiny, that history is affecting Scotland—the lairds and their way
of life are disappearing—but her focus is on the individual, not the
macrocosm.

The subject matter of Ferrier's plots resembles that of Burney,
Austen, and Edgeworth. These women wrote about what they knew
best: the education and emotional lives of women, social manners,
and the battles of the sexes. In many ways, however, Ferrier's work
is more like that of the satirists of the eighteenth century. In fact,
Ferrier irritated some critics because her novels did not maintain
the decorum considered proper for a woman writer. Her humor lacks
Austen's delicacy and approaches Smollett's comedy in its broad
caricatures of vulgarity and stupidity. As in Smollett's works, too,
there is a boisterous element in Ferrier's writing that sets her apart
from her more demure sister writers.

Clearly one cannot strictly categorize Ferrier's fiction; her work
fits into no established genre and she was not part of a literary group.
Literary historians, however, include her in the Blackwood group,
those Scottish writers who were published by William Blackwood
and who wrote for his Tory review, *Blackwood's Magazine*. Ferrier
is the only woman in the group, which included James Hogg, J.
G. Lockhart, William Edmonstone Aytoun, John Wilson ("Christopher North"), John Galt, Michael Scott, David Macbeth Moir
("Delta"), and Thomas Hamilton. There is as much sense to putting
these writers under one heading as there is to terming a group of

writers "Victorian": the Blackwood group did not have a common artistic theory as did, say, Wordsworth and Coleridge, nor a common cause. They were grouped together for convenience because they were a unique phenomenon of time and place. And the time and place, not the daily interchanges of an active group of artists, generated the similarities in their works. Their success and their similarity are partially results of the success of the Waverley Novels. In the year prior to the publication of *Waverley* the publisher Constable rejected Galt's *The Annals of the Parish* as unsuitable because it was Scottish. After 1814, publishers could not find enough Scottish novels. Readers wanted to laugh at Scottish peasants and Scottish dialect. They wanted to hear about the romantic beauty of the Highlands. Scottish writers who complied with the readers' wishes were considered part of a literary group.

In general, however, each of these writers was an individualist. Religion interested Lockhart and Hogg, as it did Ferrier, but each handled that thorny subject very differently in fiction. Lockhart and Hogg were fascinated by the darker aspects of Scottish character, although Hogg treated the subject satirically and Lockhart treated it seriously. Ferrier delighted in the humorous facets of Scottish character. In spirit her work is closer to Galt and the lesser-known Moir and Wilson. Each of them focused on Scottish regional life, depicted peasants as well as upper-class characters, and delighted in the idiosyncrasies of the Scottish personality. Unlike these male writers, Ferrier created plots concerned with young ladies who dwell in mansions and inherit fortunes; she imitated the English female novelists in her basic story lines. But her minor characters were completely her own invention, and they set her novels apart from the typical romances of her time and make her novels amusing even today.

Withering

At her best, Ferrier is funnier than Galt and equally capable of creating a well-knit scene, a memorable character, and evocative Scottish dialogue. At her worst, her work reminds us of those innumerable nineteenth-century popular novels written by "A Lady of Fashion." Her novels suffer from the flaws of many works of art that emerge in the vanguard of a movement. Although the author's voice and viewpoint are original, her works are uneven. They lack the unity and polish of later novels written to fit an already-established pattern. Later Scottish novels are often more thematically coherent and better structured than Ferrier's, but they are also less vital and original. In the wake of the great popularity of Scottish fiction, mid-nineteenth century Scottish novels were mostly hackwork aimed at a predictable audience. But, even though most of the later novels did not remain popular any longer than most best sellers do today, they helped to obscure Ferrier's less-polished works. The popularity of the Scottish novel declined quickly after the death of Scott.

By mid-century English novels had once again eclipsed Scottish fiction. Now England was blessed with unusual genius: Dickens, Thackeray, and George Eliot were writing novels that tower over almost all fiction written before or since. Each of these writers was profoundly influenced by Scott and his Scottish contemporaries, but each struck out on an individual path. Mid-century Scottish writers, lacking the breadth of vision of these English novelists, still tried variations on *Waverley* and *Marriage,* melding comic Scottish peasants, Scottish dialect, and Highland scenery in various tried-and-true permutations. Yet even these writers' works were read more than those of Susan Ferrier.

In 1883 a reviewer for *The Nation* attempted to analyze Ferrier's decline. He admits that she was more skilled than most writers of her time, standing just a "little below Miss Austen in point of humor, and Miss Edgeworth in point of wit and sterling sense."[6] But, he maintains, the novel took such enormous strides forward in the fifty years after she published that a reader could no longer enjoy her works. Writers, he claims, had acquired a subtlety of expression and plotting that Ferrier did not have. Even Charlotte Yonge—who was clearly not in Ferrier's artistic league at all—had learned to avoid "crude and platitudinous reflections"[7] and overt moralizing.

The reviewer is accurate in this part of his analysis: although moralizing had by no means disappeared from fiction, the best writers had learned more subtle means of conveying it. His second point, however, is more debatable. He claims that society had grown up: "the world in which [Ferrier] moved and for which she wrote—that is to say, the world of educated English gentlemen and English ladies—was in her day much less cultivated both in width and subtlety than is the same world in 1883."[8] Ferrier's heroines, he claims, are as complex as a contemporary child of eleven. This is by no means a new concept: every generation thinks itself more sophisticated than its predecessor. But one could quite effectively argue that in many ways the brilliant society of Edinburgh in 1800 was more vital and intellectually stimulating than mid-Victorian London. In maintaining that there are no Miss Pratts or Lady Julianas in the Britain of his time, the reviewer is doubtless accurate; but there were none in turn-of-the-century Britain either. Ferrier did not draw her characters solely from life; she flattened and foreshortened them in the time-honored tradition of satire. It was not the people in society who had changed; it was their taste in fiction.

One of the major advances in the nineteenth-century novel was realism. Many of Dickens's characters are as flat as Lady Juliana, but their world is multidimensional; theirs is not the world of pure satire. Anthony Trollope's Barsetshire is more firmly rooted in reality than is Ferrier's Glenfern Castle. Mid-Victorian readers became impatient with *Marriage* after they encountered the more complex worlds of *Middlemarch* and *Great Expectations.* In 1859 George Eliot paused, in the midst of telling the tale of *Adam Bede,* to explain that her motive in writing was to depict reality as closely as does a Dutch painting, "to give a faithful account of men and things as they have mirrored themselves in my mind."[9] Readers responded enthusiastically to this change. Simple moralizing and pure satire gave way to complex dramas of real life.

The Victorian Scottish novelists, however, did not pick up the gauntlet that George Eliot flung before them. Despite the obvious changes in their society—industrialization, progressive anglicization—they continued depicting comic and sentimental Scottish crofters and lairds. Their works were quickly categorized as the "Kailyard" (kitchen-garden) School of Scottish literature.

The only Victorian Scottish novelist to remain popular has been Robert Louis Stevenson, for he brought back some of the swashbuckling excitement that delighted readers of *Waverley.* Although he relied on some of the techniques of the Kailyard School, he created Highlanders who were not overly cute or completely romanticized. His Scotland came alive in a way that the Kailyarders' did not. His last novel, the unfinished *Weir of Hermiston,* moved him several steps above the adventures of *Treasure Island;* he did not live to attain his complete potential as a novelist. When he died in 1894, the voice of Scottish literature still had not found its way into the modern era.

New Growth

Twentieth-century Scotland, oddly enough, has produced more comic voices akin to that of Susan Ferrier than did the decades immediately following her death. Perhaps, faced with our complex world, we can enjoy again the simplicity of farce. For whatever reasons, we are blessed that writers such as Lillian Beckwith, Compton Mackenzie, and Eric Linklater have carried on and updated Scottish comedy. These modern writers may not consciously evoke the voice of *Marriage* in their works; but clearly the consistent elements of Scottish romance and humor that we find in them were derived from the Scottish consciousness and brand of comedy that Ferrier helped to popularize.

Lillian Beckwith's Bruach stories incorporate the grotesque Scottish humor and comic elements of day-to-day life that we find in Ferrier's books. Life on a Hebridean croft is in many ways more primitive than it was in Glenfern Castle, and the prim English narrator, Miss Peckwit, is as out of place as Lady Juliana. Like Ferrier, Beckwith opposes civilized English life with primitive Scottish existence, creating wonderfully incongruous scenes along the way. Beckwith follows the Scottish tendency to disassociate her settings from the industrialized world—even the installation of a telephone on Bruach is a big event. And, like Ferrier and Scott, Beckwith uses dialect with unerring effectiveness. In the letter that gives the first Bruach book its name, Morag writes: "Surely its that quiet here even the sheeps themselves on the hills is lonely and as to the sea its that near I use it myself every day for the refusals."[10]

The shift from the romantic to the prosaic exemplified in Morag's letter is vital to the texture of all the Bruach books—just as in *Destiny*, for example, we drop from an uplifting description of Highland scenery to a meal of "cocky leeky" soup, collops, and tripe. There is a Ferrier-like enjoyment of the grotesque in Beckwith too. Both can find humor in death: the peasant woman on Lord Rossmoor's estate in *The Inheritance* keeps her healthy husband's dead clothes at hand, claiming he will die at any moment. Johnny and Lachy in *The Hills is Lonely* (1959) take time from grave-digging to play skittles with the teeth of a grinning skull. Beckwith's peasants are earthier than anyone in a Ferrier novel, but the authors' black humor runs in similar veins.

Farce is linked with death in Linklater's work also. In *Ripeness is All* (1935) angry pigs tear through a garden party benefiting the Brackenshire Association for Improved Slaughterhouses. As a result of being in the rain during this chaotic scene, Lady Caroline Purefoy dies of pneumonia; we are reminded of Lord Rossmoor's death following Miss Pratt's arrival in a hearse. By counterposing sudden death with grotesque humor, both authors create a bizarre comic tension unlike the pawky or sentimental humor in the Kailyard fiction. Moreover, both of these scenes subtly convey the passing of an elite gentry: Lord Rossmoor is crushed by Miss Pratt's middle-class effrontery; Lady Caroline is destroyed by wild upheaval in the social setting she has created.

The passing of the old order and way of life is the comic fulcrum in Compton Mackenzie's Scottish farces. His mock heroes, Ben Nevis and Kilwhillie, are the "last of the lairds" in the twentieth century. Rather than fight the English, they war with the National Union of Hikers. Like Scotland itself, Ben Nevis is supported and benignly controlled by England: his rich English wife keeps him in line with her booming voice and provides the money to maintain his castle. Ferrier's Lord Rossmoor and Glenroy are the less attractive antecedents of Mackenzie's comic heroes. Land-proud, ineffectual, anachronistic, they represent a doomed class that does not recognize its obsolescence.

Clearly many of Ferrier's themes and comic strategies have endured the passing of time. Given the present popularity of Scottish farce, Ferrier's satire may be more appealing to modern readers than it was to the Victorians. Modern readers, however, are less tolerant of pious moralizing than were the devotees of Charlotte Yonge. Popular taste is unpredictable, but unless it takes an unusually extreme turn, Ferrier's three works will never appear in paperback. Nonetheless, they should not be forgotten, for from them have sprouted generations of Scottish comedy. Her novels, moreover, are original, vital, and marked with the unique stamp of a penetrating brain and a sharp, discerning eye. Like Lily Briscoe's canvasses, Ferrier's books lie dusty and unnoticed in back bedrooms; now it is time to bring them into the light.

Notes and References

Preface

1. Anand Chitnis, *The Scottish Enlightenment* (London, 1976), p. 4.
2. Augustine Birrell, "Miss Ferrier," *More Obiter Dicta* (New York, 1924), p. 32.

Chapter One

1. Henry Grey Graham, *The Social Life of Scotland in the Eighteenth Century* (London: Adam & Charles Black, 1950), p. 536.
2. James Boswell, *A Tour to the Hebrides* (New York: The Viking Press, 1936), p. 11.
3. Robert Chambers, *Traditions of Edinburgh* (London, 1868), p. 13.
4. Quoted by David Daiches, *Edinburgh* (London, 1978), p. 225.
5. Quoted by Daiches, *Edinburgh,* pp. 152–53.
6. Henry Cockburn, *Memorials of His Time,* ed. Karl F. C. Miller (Chicago, 1974), pp. 52–53.
7. Francis Watt, *The Book of Edinburgh Anecdote* (New York, 1913), p. 204.
8. Ibid., p. 207.
9. Cockburn, *Memorials,* p. 60.
10. Recounted by John Doyle, ed., in notes to Susan Ferrier's *Memoir and Correspondence* (London: Eveleigh Nash & Grayson, 1929), p. 19; hereafter cited in the text as *MC* followed by page number.
11. Cockburn, *Memorials,* pp. 60–61.

Chapter Two

1. Robert Burns, *Complete Poetical Works* (New York: Thomas Y. Crowell & Co., 1900), p. 151.
2. J. G. Lockhart, *Memoirs of the Life of Sir Walter Scott, Bart.* (Edinburgh, 1845), p. 89.

Chapter Three

1. Marion Lockhead, *The Scots Household in the Eighteenth Century* (Edinburgh, 1948), p. 247.
2. Mona Wilson, *Jane Austen and Some Contemporaries* (London, 1938), p. 133.

3. J. G. Lockhart, *Peter's Letters to His Kinfolk* (New York: Goodrich & Co., 1820), p. 167.

4. Ibid., p. 173.

5. *Marriage* (London: Eveleigh Nash & Grayson, 1929), p. 262; hereafter cited in the text as *M* followed by page number.

Chapter Four

1. Sacheverell Sitwell and Frances Bamford, *Edinburgh* (Boston, 1938), p. 289.

2. "Recollections of Visits to Ashistiel and Abbotsford," *Temple Bar* 40 (1874), p. 329; hereafter cited in the text as *R* followed by page number.

3. Quoted by Carola Oman, *The Wizard of the North* (London, 1973), p. 142.

4. Walter Scott, *Journal* (Edinburgh, 1891), p. 820.

5. Lockhart, *Sir Walter Scott,* p. 724.

6. Scott, *Journal,* p. 342.

7. Ibid., p. 635.

8. *The Inheritance* (London: Eveleigh Nash & Grayson, 1929), p. 25.

Chapter Five

1. Nancy L. Paxton, "Subversive Feminism: A Reassessment of Susan Ferrier's *Marriage,*" *Women and Literature* 6, no. 1 (1976):19.

2. Walter Scott, *The Legend of Montrose* (London and New York: George Routledge & Sons, 1879), p. 339.

3. W. M. Parker, *Susan Ferrier and John Galt* (London, 1965), p. 22.

4. Quoted by Aline Grant, *Susan Ferrier of Edinburgh* (Denver, 1957), p. 108.

5. Anon., "Miss Ferrier's Novels," *Edinburgh Review* 74 (1841–42):498.

6. Anon., "Miss Ferrier," *Macmillan's Magazine* 79 (1898–99):419.

7. Wendy Craik, "Susan Ferrier," *Scott Bicentenary Essays,* ed. Alan Bell (Edinburgh, 1973), p. 322.

8. Anon., "Miss Ferrier's Novels," *Edinburgh Review,* p. 499.

9. Ibid.

10. Ibid., p. 501.

11. George Saintsbury, "Miss Ferrier," *Collected Essays and Papers,* vol. 1 (London, 1923), p. 314.

12. Craik, "Susan Ferrier," p. 326.

13. Ibid., p. 323.

14. Paxton, "Subversive Feminism," p. 27.
15. Vineta Colby, *Yesterday's Women* (Princeton, 1974), pp. 98–108.

Chapter Six

1. "Miss Ferrier's Novels," *Edinburgh Review*, pp. 502–3.
2. Oliver Elton, *A Survey of English Literature, 1780–1830,* vol. 1 (London, 1912), pp. 367–68.
3. Craik, "Susan Ferrier," p. 324.
4. *The Inheritance* (London: Eveleigh Nash & Grayson, 1929), p. 551. All page numbers in the text of this chapter refer to this volume.
5. F. R. Hart, *The Scottish Novel* (Cambridge, Mass., 1978), p. 61.
6. Colby, *Yesterday's Women*, p. 100.
7. Ibid., p. 101.
8. Hart, *The Scottish Novel*, p. 63.

Chapter Seven

1. John Wilson [Christopher North], "Noctes Ambrosianae," no. 58, *Blackwood's* 30 (1831):553.
2. "Miss Ferrier," *Edinburgh Review*, p. 504.
3. "Miss Ferrier," *Macmillan's*, p. 425.
4. Saintsbury, "Miss Ferrier," p. 324.
5. Craik, "Susan Ferrier," p. 328.
6. Saintsbury, "Miss Ferrier," p. 325.
7. Hart, *The Scottish Novel*, pp. 64–65.
8. *Destiny* (London: Eveleigh Nash & Grayson, 1929), p. 33. All page numbers in the text of this chapter refer to this volume.
9. Hart, *The Scottish Novel*, p. 67.
10. Ibid., p. 65.
11. Ibid., p. 66.

Chapter Eight

1. Anna Laetitia Barbauld, "On Education," *Works*, vol. 2 (London: Longman, Hurst, et al., 1825), pp. 318–19.
2. Maria Edgeworth, *Patronage*, vol. 3 (London: Baldwin & Cradoch, 1833), p. 78.
3. Charlotte Bury, *Conduct is Fate*, vol. 1 (Edinburgh: William Blackwood, 1822), pp. 131–32.
4. Quoted by Wilson, *Jane Austen and Some Contemporaries*, p. 69.

Chapter Nine

1. Hart, *The Scottish Novel*, p. 4.
2. Ibid., p. 8.

3. David Craig, *Scottish Literature and the Scottish People, 1680–1830* (London, 1961), p. 215.

4. Kurt Wittig, *The Scottish Tradition in Literature* (Edinburgh, 1958), p. 245.

5. Lockhart, *Sir Walter Scott,* p. 618.

6. Anon., "Miss Ferrier's Novels," *The Nation* 37 (1883):233.

7. Ibid.

8. Ibid.

9. George Eliot, *Adam Bede* (Boston: Houghton Mifflin Co., 1968), p. 150.

10. Lillian Beckwith, *The Hills is Lonely* (London: Arrow Books, 1977), p. 11.

Selected Bibliography

PRIMARY SOURCES

Destiny. 3 vols. Edinburgh: Cadell, 1831.
The Inheritance. 3 vols. Edinburgh: Blackwood, 1824.
Marriage. 3 vols. Edinburgh: Blackwood, 1818.
Memoir and Correspondence. Edited by John Doyle. London: J. Murray, 1898.
"Recollections of Visits to Ashistiel and Abbotsford." *Temple Bar* 40 (1874):329–35.
Works. 4 vols. London: Eveleigh Nash & Grayson, 1929.

SECONDARY SOURCES

1. Books
Chambers, Robert. *Traditions of Edinburgh.* London: W. & R. Chambers, 1868. An anecdotal history of Edinburgh focusing on the eighteenth century.
Chitnis, Anand. *The Scottish Enlightenment.* London: Croom Helm, 1976. A social history of Scotland from the mid-eighteenth century to the mid-nineteenth century.
Cockburn, Henry. *Memorials of His Time.* Edited by Karl F. C. Miller. Chicago: University of Chicago Press, 1974. An autobiographical retrospective of Edinburgh from the 1790s to 1830.
Colby, Vineta. *Yesterday's Women.* Princeton: Princeton University Press, 1974. An intelligent analysis of Ferrier's interest in education of the heart. Also discusses Barbauld, Austen, Edgeworth, and others.
Craig, David. *Scottish Literature and the Scottish People, 1680–1830.* London: Chatto & Windus, 1961. Valuable standard volume. Little on Ferrier, but much information on the Scottish reading public, Scottish language, Scottish religion, and other topics related to a study of Scottish literature.
Daiches, David. *Edinburgh.* London: Hamish Hamilton, 1978. A short, readable history of Edinburgh from earliest times to the present.
———. *The Paradox of Scottish Culture.* London: Oxford University Press, 1964. Daiches does not discuss Ferrier, but he analyzes the eighteenth-

century experience in Scotland, the institutions, and the city of Edinburgh.

Douglas, Sir George. *The Blackwood Group*. Edinburgh: Oliphant, Anderson & Ferrier, 1897. Surveys Ferrier's life and works as well as those of her contemporaries in the Blackwood Group.

Elton, Oliver. *A Survey of English Literature, 1780–1830*. Vol. 1. London: Edward Arnold, 1912. Overview of Ferrier. Discusses her "sense of surface absurdities."

Graham, Henry Grey. *The Social Life of Scotland in the Eighteenth Century*. London: Adam & Charles Black, 1950. First published in 1899, this volume offers a comprehensive view of life in rural Scotland, Edinburgh, and Glasgow from 1700 to 1800.

Grant, Aline. *Susan Ferrier of Edinburgh*. Denver: Alan Swallow, 1957. The only book-length biography of Ferrier, the volume contains a sizable amount of information without footnotes. The book is readable, but not scholarly.

Hamilton, Catherine J. *Women Writers: Their Works and Ways*. New York: Books for Libraries Press, 1971. This reprint of the 1892 edition offers basic biographical information on Ferrier and other nineteenth-century women writers. Does not include footnotes.

Hart, F. R. *The Scottish Novel*. Cambridge: Harvard University Press, 1978. The most complete book on the Scottish novel, this provides incisive analysis of Ferrier's works. Discusses her values of "local piety, traditional community, and the tranquility of provincial withdrawal."

Jack, Ian. *English Literature, 1815–1832*. Oxford: Clarendon Press, 1963. Discusses Ferrier in a chapter entitled, "John Galt and the Minor Writers of Prose Fiction."

Johnson, R. Brimley. *The Women Novelists*. Glasgow: W. Collins Sons & Co., 1918. Survey of Ferrier's works. Describes her as a follower of Burney, not Austen.

Lindsay, Maurice. *History of Scottish Literature*. London: Robert Hale, 1977. Discusses Ferrier in his survey of nineteenth-century Scottish novelists, but includes more quotation than analysis.

Lockhart, J. G. *Memoirs of the Life of Sir Walter Scott, Bart*. Edinburgh: Robert Cadell, 1845. Only a few characteristic vignettes about Ferrier, but many personal views of Edinburgh and its inhabitants as well as of Scott himself.

Lockhead, Marion. *The Scots Household in the Eighteenth Century*. Edinburgh: Moray Press, 1948. Detailed study of all aspects of Scottish domestic life in different social spheres and parts of the country.

Oman, Carola. *The Wizard of the North*. London: Hodder and Stoughton, 1973. A biography of Walter Scott that describes many literary figures of the time.

Parker, W. M. *Susan Ferrier and John Galt.* London: Longmans, Green & Co., 1965. A good introduction to Ferrier and Galt in pamphlet form. Includes brief bibliography and critiques of their works.

Scott, Sir Walter. *Journal.* Edinburgh: David Douglas, 1891. Includes anecdotes about Ferrier and her father and much material on the literary characters of the time.

Sitwell, Sacheverell, and Francis Bamford. *Edinburgh.* Boston: Houghton Mifflin Co., 1938. An overview of Edinburgh history from earliest times to 1822.

Spacks, Patricia Meyer. *The Female Imagination.* New York: Alfred A. Knopf, 1975. Does not mention Ferrier in particular, but analyzes themes and images that recur throughout fiction written by women.

Watt, Francis. *The Book of Edinburgh Anecdote.* New York: Charles Scribner's Sons, 1913. An amusing, gossipy collection of stories about Edinburgh personalities through the centuries.

Wilson, Mona. *Jane Austen and Some Contemporaries.* London: Cresset Press, 1938. Does not discuss Ferrier, but includes some worthwhile material on Eliza Fletcher, Mary Somerville, and other Scottish and English women of the time. Does not include footnotes.

Wittig, Kurt. *The Scottish Tradition in Literature.* Edinburgh: Oliver & Boyd, 1958. Although this work barely mentions Ferrier, it provides a good overview of Scottish literature from earliest times.

Young, Douglas. *Edinburgh in the Age of Sir Walter Scott.* Norman: University of Oklahoma Press, 1965. An introduction to early nineteenth-century Edinburgh. Does not mention Ferrier.

2. Articles

Birrell, Augustine. "Miss Ferrier." *More Obiter Dicta.* New York: Charles Scribner's Sons, 1924, pp. 30–35. Includes a conversational review of *Memoir and Correspondence of Susan Ferrier.* Mourns the waning popularity of her works and the passing of a way of life.

Bushnell, Nelson S. "Susan Ferrier's *Marriage* as Novel of Manners." *Studies in Scottish Literature* 5, no. 4 (1968):216–28. An intelligent analysis of differences in English and Scottish manners as Ferrier dramatizes and satirizes them.

Craik, Wendy. "Susan Ferrier." *Scott Bicentenary Essays.* Edited by Alan Bell. Edinburgh: Scottish Academic Press, 1973. On Ferrier's comedy. Craik views her as a primitive embarking on new methods.

"Miss Ferrier." *Macmillan's Magazine* 79 (1898–99):419–27. Provides overview of her works. States that her concern with moral instruction has proved her downfall in terms of long-lasting reader appeal.

"Miss Ferrier's Novels." *Edinburgh Review* 74 (1841–42):498–505. Reviews 1841 edition of novels "in cheap and popular form." Praises

Ferrier excessively, placing her on a level with Austen and assuring us that her works will outlive Scott's.

"Miss Ferrier's Novels." *The Nation* 37 (1883):230–32. Discusses why Ferrier's works seem dated and why novels have changed so much in fifty years.

"Miss Ferrier's Novels." *Temple Bar* 54 (1878):308–28. Reviews principally the creation of *Marriage* through the Ferrier-Clavering correspondence.

Paxton, Nancy L. "Subversive Feminism: A Reassessment of Susan Ferrier's *Marriage.*" *Women and Literature* 6, no. 1 (1976):18–29. Interesting but extreme analysis of Ferrier as a "subversive" feminist.

Saintsbury, George. "Miss Ferrier." *Collected Essays and Papers,* Vol. I. London: J. M. Dent & Sons, 1923, pp. 302–29. Discusses each of Ferrier's works, commenting on the eccentricities of the fictional characters which contribute to the lack of balance as well as the humor in the works. Includes a comparison with Austen and Edgeworth.

Wilson, John [Christopher North]. "Noctes Ambrosianae." No. 58. *Blackwood's* 30 (1831):531–45. Discusses Ferrier's merits: praises the scene in which Ronald returns to his family in *Destiny* and commends her portrait of the last Scottish lairds.

Index